GHOST ROMANCE, A COMEDY MELEE

illustrated

Keith Hulse

ISBN 9798402217904
Cover design by: Art Painter
Library of Congress Control Number: 2018675309
Printed in the United States of America

Dedicated to the ghosts, wildlife, food, and an Island named Borneo.

"What, no you misunderstand, I am Peter," but he could call himself 'Handsome Prince Charming,' they still would rob, beat, steal his clothes, especially the stilettos and leave him in his lingerie's, as night workers were hygienic and did not wear another's unmentionables. And Steve went off behind the bushes with these two-night workers and the question is? Did Steve have rabies from a monkey eaten by a leopard and did he offer a packet of crispy chili roasted crickets to these girls, and another question, what explosive reply did these girls give him, our 'Igor' of the story.?

CONTENTS

FOREWORD

The story teller was an archaeologist, soldier, jack of all trades, and now Vereran Scottish Warblinded and artist.

He gets visits from spirit people, he is not a medium, just ghosts spirit people like him.

His house is full of cats, spirit folk love cats?

INTRODUCTION

Subject matter is laughable ghosts.
They walk beside you and not seen,
unless they want you to,
then can become right pests.

This story revolves round lonely Henry, a ghost stuck in Borneo.
Until Lizzy the vet arrives and Henry and his friend, Calamity
the ape spend their whole story rescuing her from Roger, a vil-
lain as story needs one.
And a clown, Steve who doubles as Igor the monster, as works
unpaid for Peter another bad folk.
What a chase, from Lizzy's apartment to the zoo to the outback,
where aliens take them captive.
Yes, every story needs an alien abduction.
Aliens that might be under your bed waiting for you to sleep,
then whisk you to Mars.
Men readers, the alien crew was 99% girls.
If a girl reader, one alien male stuffed in leopard print 'Y' fronts.
Really unbelievable good madcap rubbish, aliens and ghosts do
not exist.
Sweet dreams, bye.

PREFACE

This story is intended to bring laughter into a sad world.
To encourage the idea ghosts, aliens, exist, then so does an After Life.
Rejoice then,
there are parallel universes.
Live a good life then,
see you over there, I a might be your employer so, read the book as ghosts have long memories.

PROLOGUE

See Peter grew up with, stories of antiheroes, of men who stole, murdered, and pimped. Nothing about good folk, so looked up to madams, and not angelic father figures. Whereas other children had Goldilocks, Shrek, Peter Rabbit and Super Man, poor Peter had peasant folklore about were-wolves, Frankenstein the Monster, and Russian Big Foot tales, and a fear of darkened spaces, so much he pushed himself to become a young God-father. Instead of horse heads he put crocodile heads in people's beds to lubricate them into paying protection cash.

Unfortunately, a handful of crocodiles were still alive, that was bad for business.

Ghost Romance, a Comedy

BY

Keith Hulse

54891

lugbooks@gmail.com

Lugbooks.co.uk

Table of Contents

[CHAPTER 1] — A LONELY GHOST

Figure 1 A 1905 photo Henry Adamson

1921: I am Henry Adamson, a zoologist, who once upon a time, worked on the big Island of Borneo, and I am a ghost, so the former is all past tense. How can a ghost be a zoologist, well those are my memories, now helping my friend Steve Jones catch butterflies to sketch, then paint with watercolor what he drew? Beautiful animals, with long black tails, big too.

Why draw, he has this avoidance about pinning butterflies to a board for a museum. He also felt murderous when standing on a plant, on slow creepy crawlies, and in the jungle that meant he danced along jungle paths avoiding red ants and such, wanting to crawl up legs, then bite. Snakes waited to bite you to, so you died. Think he missed their strikes as sang happy melodies that his feet matched the notes. Twirling in the air, his head peering into bush life, a tree snake startled, back venom fangs, and he was gone as it chewed leaves where he had been.

"Hiss," the snake spitting out disgusting chloroform tasting green stuff, and then vomited, that fell upon the slither below taking aim at a descending Steve, so missed and struck what dung beetles were pushing.

Oh, lovely, formidable the jungle was a lively place. Why look at the snake above, fleeing from angry leaf cutter ants, them that sew up leaves, and that was their creation the snake messed up, REVENGE was on their antennae.

And below, the slither now covered in annoyed dung beetles,

that was their dinner, lunch, and breakfast the slither just ruined, so wanted REVENGE.

Did Steve sing songs from 'Jungle Book?' That would be stealing from your imagination! More from his nursery days, of happiness when babysitter bent over to change his diaper, and Steve ogled, and ogled in nursery, and ogled in primary school, and ogled in secondary school and in university joined the 'OGLE SOCIETY,' a bird watching front for the birds they ogled were human.

So, ogling Steve sang rude ditties disguised as innocent children songs leaping about with a butterfly net. A man happy in his work, a kind-hearted soul who picked worms out of jungle footprints rained filled in case they drowned.

A man who climbed up hundred-foot trees to put back a baby bird fallen from a nest.

A hundred feet of dodging orangutangs annoyed at his feet trampling about their nests, avoiding tree snakes that avoided him as remembered ants and dung beetles, avoiding monkeys that imitated him climbing, hoping he did fall bouncing off every tree branch and lie prone on the jungle track till a tiger came, then be eaten all up.

What loathsome little monkeys, yes, monkeys fed up with humans catching them and taking them to LABORATORIES, they wanted REVENGE.

 Steve wishing the buzzing mosquitoes away but loved him so, stayed as he had a reputation amongst them that he would not use a DDT spray; was against his belief; "poor little midges," he muttereth, as Steve was unhinged by the jungle slithers. The midges were the true murderers spreading malaria, yellow fever, and insanity from the urge to scratch a thousand bites; so, when we slept in tents, was not snores keeping you woken, but folks scratching. 'Scratch here and a scratchy there, Old MacDonald had a farm,' well a ghost can be musical? Who is the ghost, Henry Adamson as now a hundred years and more have passed since 1905?

Now Steve, who is physically alive, sat on a fold down chair on a wharf in *Sandakan, 2021, waiting for a small cargo ship to arrive. In my days, a sailing ship or paddle steamer, how time flies just like these big blue dragon flies about him, feeding on mosquitoes resting on his chair, digesting the blood meal Steve gave? A slug had managed to reach his neck, their eyes met, then Steve ate it in one swallow.

Nearby folk asked, "Did that man juts eat a slug, only a mad person did do that, that is Steve the explorer?"

(* Sandakan, Northeast Borneo looking out into green hot seas where giant squids live.)

And white pelicans landed in the sea as a sea plane circled to land behind the steamer.

On board the cargo ship was new help for Steve, a New York vet from Central Zoo, yes, the one Alex the Lion came from, come to check it was not Steve sending caged animals in small spaces, a cruelty matter, someone was trading them to American markets?

That vet did not know Steve Jones, whoever wrote 'Fierce Animals,' must have met Steve, why his tent was full of cuddly furry thingumabobs; the bigger man eaters he wisely avoided; but there were jars full of insects, slugs, and parts of teddy bears?

I am afraid, Steven had lost his mind as the jungle claimed his mind as REVENGE, and I cared for him as he was kind, but this slug eating was new?

Beside him stood a ghost, his carer , me, Henry Adamson from Shetland. It was a pity he did not know I was there; well only handfuls of physicals can see spirit folk? They say one in a thousand has mediumistic gifts, guess what, Steve was ordinary, but not the rainbow-colored butterflies he caught and photo-graphed, they were extraordinary, beautiful. Steven Jones would try and give the goldfish 'resuscitation, a truly kind physical.

A goldfish was not a slug so was safe. Yes, I still looked upon this physical Steve as a friend as his core was kind. I heard crunching, yes, so looked the other way, to look was to confirm Steve had lost his sanity. "Lovely roach delicious," Steven wiping ketchup from his fingers.

"REVENGE" the jungle cried out, "REVENGE."

How could this living person be my friend? To answer we play a game, when did I die? I arrived in Sandakan by paddle steamer, it still had sea crocodiles sunning on the estuary banks, the ships anchored where pirate.

The British navy were here, they knew that noisy lot playing mah-jongg were the pirates but had to wait till they went to sea to sink them, also had to wait till Jack Tars recovered from malaria.

And Eddy was King Emperor and the 2nd Boer War ended 1902.

Now the answer to my ghostly game, oh yes, the ghost of an orangutan stood next to me, it held onto me, great apes are not good walkers even in The After Life, still has memories of tree living. The ape was a friend too, with a sane mind for spirits can think, no idea how?

Is 1905, Sandakan market, Borneo, got murdered musing over buying Clay Pot Soup, a prawn mixture, was hungry so never noticed the murderers close on me; either did the food seller, she had her hand out for cash, so when the wire went about my throat and pulled, I fell back kicking the hot cauldron of soup over two attackers, who cares about them, assassins they were. "Charlie Chan, go home now or I tell your mum, do what auntie tells you," the vendor recognizing one.

Another one slipped on the spilled ingredients and as he fell stretched out a hand just as a fish monger was chopping fish heads off. Oh, it was nasty and never mind a hungry stray dog gobbled the fingers so felt loved by heaven, for it says, 'God feeds the birds of the air and the lilies of the field.'

"Cousin Woo, your fingers, but what are doing with triads?" The fish monger asked.

"Hey, who is paying for the soup?" The lady vendor. A shiny coin was flicked her way by an unknown.

"Not enough," as she haggled with the unknown, adding, "That is more like it," the lady vendor accepting five coins and 'never saw nothing'.

It was food off putting, what happened to me, the police said were thieves whose robbery went wrong, sarcasm needed here, they stabbed me vigorously a hundred times to make sure I was dead, the belligerent hooligans.

And my Clay Pot Soup was smashed into pottery fragments and because the hoods wore flip flops cut their feet, a little justice, so many diseases on the street, tetanus, gangrene for instance.

I was dead all right, could say they dismembered me, that makes it gruesome. A ghoulish looking spirit off 'To the Land of Faraway' where spirit people party, not breed, but are young again, and I am one of them here storifying you into believing, LIFE EXISTS AFTER DEATH, and spirits can be romantically inclined with physicals; why mention this, because it happens, and I did like to try.

I am a ghost called, mm, forgot my name, been dead a while, Henry Adamson from Shetland.

Guess what, in the spirit realm was told my murderers were hired assassins, well who wanted to murder a poor zoologist whose belongings included another pair of shorts, shirts, boots and my digging trowel? My answer tells you to burn off red Chinese spirit cash, I am penniless in spirit, believe that and believe cows jump over the moon. I am rich as Spirit is an energy giving source, makes you young again.

Also, since I am mischievous, I had better be careful that you do not label me Poltergeist, but all I am doing is expressing my humor, the joy of being alive, allowed to keep that. I did not take the great ape over, she just turned up eating a spirit honeycomb over here.

Staring at me with big ogling eyes, "Ook," which means anything, like meow, "NO, you ape me wolf," I sternly replied; well, it worked I felt so sorry, now she is my companion. "Ook," loudly that makes me think I was' had, taken in' by this ape eating banana who doubles as a server as she pours me a double spirit gin.

You can call me dead and look at my grave, but I am alive, made of energy, pure, indestructible, all living thingamabobs are made of it. Modern paranormal folks say we spirits are electromagnetic energy, well, I do not know, I am just a ghost, male, unattached and handsome and can make myself humongous places as all is about MIND here, ladies" hello," and exercise my eyebrows in invitation.

"Ook," the ape puckering lips accepting, and I behave as afraid of those drooling lips.

Go read *Ecclesiastes, a wisdom book of the Torah and sometimes Bible. Well, I am here to tell my story, not be involved in metaphysics and electro chemistry discussions as to the composition of Spirit. *Books of Wisdom include Psalms, makes them old, why full of life experiences, hence wisdom, but I have wisdom so now listen to my story and find it.

Now, a man called Mr. Roger Dee Jong, a free-lance journalist wanting fame, having found out I had stumbled across Ramapithecus bones in an old quarry made my acquaintance. Who is Ramapithecus, an early ape like creature on our ancestral line? Just look at Calamity and you have an idea as to looks.

"Ook," the ape trying to walk upright and because she is a ghost did to prove her humanity to me, so I would marry her, "No, no, no, you ape me King."

Now Roger smoked out rooms with cigar, so was shouting, 'I do not care if your clothes smell of smoke,' so should have avoided him. I did not, so stank Cuban. He was not alone, after dinner out came the Havanans and 'puff' the men.

I had met this journalist Roger, waiting for me in the Hotel Seafront, to sell the story of Ramapithecus, Roger knew I had the bones, why, because I was Mr. Nice guy, when he was visiting my camp told him what I had found. To him it was his ticket out of the East Indies, to me, back to the quarry where I had found the jawbone with teeth.

I did be famous too, I did get a job in the British Museum, salary, house, future, a wife, kids, dog and cat, live-in babysitter and house cleaners, a butler. The pets did have intestinal worms, a budgie in a cage allowed to fly about the house; is all right, the downstairs house cleaners did run about with newspaper for droppings. A big back garden full of sweet peas, mm, the smell of those purple, blue and white flowers, so sickly. And part of the garden left wild, overgrown so hedgehogs thrived, crows nesting above and, in the shadows, yellow foxy eyes.

The front garden manicured so no passing neighbor could complain about that nutty explorer living here. I did have beehives to keep burglars away, a bear manikin as a hat, coat, umbrella stand, grinning and in pin stripe trousers with braces because nude did cause offence; but big those places to cause comment in a giant cod piece.

Me, the explorer of the day, Ramapithecus was my passport to the above, instead the ape man got me chopped up, mixed with diced carrots, and fried noodles and given to the sea crocodiles, seen as personifications of the sea god Dovar Ollar.

To Roger, a job on the De Tele Graaf, a paper back in the Netherlands, why there, his father was Dutch, his mother with a 'Roger,' other name, of English descent.

Famous he did get a penthouse in Amsterdam, never marry, no kids, no dog, or wormy cats, just women and deny the offspring were his.

We were different as Blue Cheese and Cheddar.

I was nice he was bad; he hired those assassins to kill me, pretending to be after my wallet. What wallet, I was always penniless, so got stabbed a hundred times. Now the police should have guessed someone really wanted me DEAD. Who told me how I died, Captain Fokker a ghost, he came out of the old European cemetery with ninety ghosts to watch, say hello, which is dozens of onlookers and one way to die in Borneo?

Roger DeJong paid the police off, it was hot, humid, and toilets poisonous snake ridden, and the interior full of headhunters, so sensible corrupt people tried to amass a fortune to get back to Europe, or even better, Singapore or Hong Kong where money lasted while you lived as Royalty, when it ran out, immigration threw you out.

So, when I died, I saw my life replay, say happens when you enter The Light, living restfully with family members and then these 'SUPERIOR BEINGS,' come and forcibly take you to watch, 'life replay,' making you squirm over the seedy parts. I am lucky, have no seedy parts. I am linen washed of finest Egyptian cotton made spirit orb.

This 'bad life' replay would apply to Roger DeJong's, "Did I write that bad report in the South China Morning Post, so she never got employed, because she refused my dinner date?" DeJong with these beings, thinking escape as he sensed big trouble.

"Yes, you did," a Superior Being making DeJong watch, so after seeing and hearing all the harmful stuff, he felt remorseful, well what these SUPERIOR BEINGS did next was sneaky, they took him screaming to Earth, all his road paths, actors to meet, the works, well, I never got that far to' replay my life.'

Lighten up, early Christians till the Empress Theodora believed in reincarnation, 561 A.D. approx. As for Roger he escaped into The Ether to roam the darkness till eternity and make my ghostly life a hell.

It happened thus:

I lay still, dead as soggy rice to accompany your half cooked battered chicken. But was dead, above my body, dark space, no sounds, no horrid murderers, no witnesses as I was seen as an overlord, tax gatherer, European whatever just got his deserts.

Bats flew overhead as was night, their rabid saliva fell earthwards. "Kiss me baby," a lover with a gaping mouth just as the rabid infection dropped in. **REVENGE** the jungle was having.

Then I slowly focused on a crowd of curious folk, good people who sold nice food at stalls, a murder was a murder, I had witnesses, until someone said, "I know this man, he drinks with the triad, maybe into opium grown in the interior, better be careful you are not next," Mr. Roger DeJong making sure no one spoke up, they did not want those stray Chow dogs eating their murdered remains.

"Get," it was a police officer, well at least the dogs did, not Roger DeJong as he lurked hearing news.

He was a slimy, slithery, smooth-spoken man, who knew assassins.

Well, guess you think I was a character while alive the way I automatic author this story, well women said I was 'trouble' amongst themselves so avoided me, they just fantasized as bored.

"Is that me, really, that gore, me?" I asked floating about the murder scene.

No answer from the darkness except stray Chow dogs loitering growled.

The crowd knew animals saw ghosts, slowly they began to clear, later they lit joysticks and burnt red ghost paper money, to help me, so not to haunt them; except that money bought nothing here; their thoughtful prayers helped, telling demons that separated me from The Light to stay away.

Business was good for the stall sellers, but ghosts were not or mangy dogs.

"Hello Roger?" I said to him, but ignored, I was fresh out of my body, "Hello Roger, it is me," high pitched, feeling hurt, he was being rude, "Hello Roger," I lowered my voice deeply, ignored, I wanted to take small backward steps into oblivion hoping I had not been observed as so embarrassed.

Ok, my backward steps took me at a fast speed into those dogs, did they go crazy over me.

Snap tear, bite up there, pull down here, and felt nothing, they were eating spirit, ha, I had one over them, so made rude faces making them fight around De Jong who was afraid of rabies.

I needed a mirror, so left the dogs and went to a stall, they sold grannies here if you wanted a human cooker, so found a mirror.

I saw a mist melting into a white orb, me, I had limbs, feet, tummy, but not outside the mirror. Sadly, the mirror vendor saw me in the mirror and ran off screaming.

Others joined her looking in my direction.

Now, boring as reality sunk in where was my physical body, my hanging parts? Then saw the remains, **so shrieked**, the dogs were eating them, so howled and Christians in the crowd crossed themselves; I had been heard.

Other said local prayers and took out charms.

"That cannot be me?" I shouted in C minor and sat beside what remained of physical me. A dog gave a burp of satisfaction.

Horseshoe bats flew overhead, a vampire bat joined them from the jungle unnoticed.

Remaining dogs chewing interesting organs growled at my presence, a lit joystick was thrown at them, a dog howled, so ran to the fringe of the crowd, then smartly revengefully attacked hanging onto a man's trousers, and as he struggled the trousers disintegrated and folks gaped, he was wearing lingerie, suspenders, and such, in pink too.

His secret was out and not incredibly lucky this was a Muslim Sultanate.

"I am a Buddhist," he shouted vanishing in the crowd. An effeminate person smiled and slyly followed.

Someone yelped as the revengeful dog full of confidence tried her luck stealing a cooked duck from another vendor. The yelp came from the dog as out of luck as a boot stuck somewhere on its anatomy. "You again, I know you are not Cousin Cheung reincarnated, get lost," the chicken vendor. See, as a ghost I see animal spirits and like the living have personalities and this one had a hankering for cooked chicken Chinese style, and been here so often, everyone knew it as a dog, not Cheung, he hated chicken.

What am I doing, this is my gore, so stood and zoomed about a hundred feet up?

I met night jars eating mosquitoes and moths, the bats were way below, above me a moon, below Roger DeJong disappearing, heading towards the seafront. I headed to him, overshooting him, so he shivered, and half a mile down the road I stopped amongst trash were rats stood their ground, they had seen ghosts before, since I was not annoying them, they went back to eating banana skins, fried Mie Goreng, Kalimantan, grilled spicy chicken, Babi guling, whole roasted hog, and licked up Chinese curry, these vermin lived good, while out on the streets human beggars joyed when donated a copper for a bowl of rice, just rice.

Leaving the feeding fat rats, I drifted away, now where was Roger, no idea, just crowds and red juice spat out, betel nut chewing.

"I seem to be able to fly," I told myself so swam like a fish up and yes, there Roger was, all I had to do was wait.

"Wait," I told myself but swam to him, why was he solid and

me, a transparent mist?

Think I was mist, I was nothing, NOTHINGNESS, it shocks my mind and by the time I settled, Roger DeJong was gone again.

"Argh," I screamed.

Passing folk stopped and looked about for a murder, cool, wonderous, I had been heard.

I had to repeat floating, where was he? At this time, I had no suspicion he was my murderer, just that he could help me. Gone into Hotel Seafront, cool, I know that place, my hotel in town so went there, at high speed, had to control this as went right through the building and on the way out saw DeJong.

He was at my room door, illegally opening it, I did not know journalists could do that.

Oh, was I glad I kept a tidy room, no smudged underwear about or sweat ridden vests, I travelled light see as owned little? A vampire bat waited for darkness hanging from gutterin outside.

Roger looked everywhere, under bed, in closets, veranda, for what? What did I own that he wanted, Ramapithecus of course?

My casts of what bones found, the jaw, ten teeth, bit of cranium, a toe, vertebrae, where back at camp, but he did not know that ha, ha?

So, he left, and I took the shortcut, out the window so was waiting for him as he came out.

"Clear off, this is my place," a ghost, a British Jack Tar who sat begging. People ignored him, they could not see him, that meant I was not seen.

I did not want to ask why; the answer was **deadly?**

There was no time to chat, DeJong was melting in the night crowd, this town never slept.

Now DeJong organized quickly, he stopped in a Chinese Teahouse and after speaking to residents, they left. They looked like my murderers, well the black loose clothes did, all had Black Hoods to hide the face, and following arrived on a small river boat, wood fired, room for Roger, where he got comfortable, at his feet a canvas bag with my remains, crocodile food, not a trace of me would remain, I never existed in Sandakan or in his mind.

I wondered how safe DeJong was, hired hungry sea crocodiles following, following cooked chicken pieces tossed them by the Black Hooded ones, hired to eat me.

I knew where they were going, my camp, see, a mile down, about thirty, disembark and go in land avoiding leeches, about ten miles, and my camp ha, ha, not funny now.

(Well, I did never get any visitors if told the truth, forty miles upriver? Forty miles of orchids and loud insect noises, big hairy spiders dropping onto you, leeches on your bum. No wonder I was lonely "Ook," "No not you, go away, here a banana, fetch.)

None of the badmen saw me, on the boat my orb was missed because the night sky was full of twinkling stars, and the river yellow crocodile eyes waiting for someone to slip in. Even when they made their way inland, no one noticed me, fireflies about, and poisonous snakes, never jungle walk at night so explains why one of Roger's men jumped screaming. The others passed him; his share was now theirs.

"Do not leave me," he shouted in Malay, see automatically translated on my side; but they did and as he is jumping about holding an ankle toppled over and landed on what bit him.

"Bad snake," I hissed at it in snake language, "Hiss," a reply, "Oh, your wife bit him, and now you have bitten him three times for good measure, ok, hiss, bye," and went after DeJong.

"Hiss," the snakes biting a fourth time, it wanted RE-VEVENGE, 'Uncle Slither' ended up as human gall Bladder soup.

De Jong lost two more men: the non- martial artists up

front with machetes cutting away creepers fallen onto the track. There was no anti venom those days, he left one man to help them back to the boat, hungry crocodiles waited on the sand. Boy, girl crocodiles, does not matter, wanting a meal.

Now a brawl as my security personnel resisted DeJong, it was the way he marched in demanding, then setting his lads to ransack. Yes, I helped my folk, I orbed in front of those fisting or wielding a knife, so momentarily blinded, and fisted in return. I was new to this so did not know what I could do? My fist went through them, and with shivers returned to killing my folks. One of the baddies shivered so much he pooped and ran off into the jungle, never to be seen again, jungle REVENGE.

The roar of a tiger deafened so all fighting stopped, then a tiger belched, the signal to continue killing.

My security personnel were local volunteer laborer's, paid with food and shelter and X rated postcards, I really needed a woman, so did they, they could sell those post cards then visit the back door of The Sea Front Hotel, to buy expensive clothes pegs?

"You know what this is?" DeJong pulling a small black handgun from a pocket of a white stained jacket, yellow with sweat. Briefly essence of unwashed arm pits was smelled by all, confirming the opinion that Europeans never washed, especially their underwear, why stank of sour milk.

A hidden orange orangutan watched him from the jungle, it had been asleep dreaming of a mate.

Well, my remaining living laborers backed to the edge of the jungle, merging with it, swallowed by darkness, the orangutan said nothing.

De Jong shot about the jungle, moans replied, he did need to make sure survivors starved. That explains why he looted my camp of condensed milk, carnation milk, bags of tea, rice, toilet paper, water, that precious commodity he took all, even pillows, now his men were loaded with supplies and of my bones, he buried, in a spot X, he did be back, alone. He was my murderer.

The orangutan slumped dead, DeJong had shot it, a lucky hit between the eyes. The body fell into the gaping mouth of a crocodile that went back to the depths of the river. Which reptile ate the ape, there where hundreds of crocodiles, who knows?

"Hello," I said to the ape spirit, it looked at me, grinned then went to The Light through a tunnel of Sparkles, impressive, The Light pulled at me, but allowed me to stay?

Fruit bats flew disturbed, so noisy and dropping stuff, Roger in retaliation fired shots up.

How did Roger kill his men off, the snakes got two and the crocodiles those at the boat, well he needed the rest to store his loot in a Godown, everyone has access to one here, for sea chest storage and Egyptian mummies, that is me again, see some spirits are just 100% proof, like me, so be careful how much you believe my story; all true, not a porker told.

Roger DeJong took his men out again, back to my camp to look for survivors to murder. He found no one, they had decided to follow the river down-stream to Sandakan, through mangroves where Bull Shark babies and mothers waited, poison-colored snakes hung from branches to bite your neck, army ants from nowhere swarmed up your legs and ate your bits so you jumped, well, you did fall once your legs were bones, a lot of bones in this story.

DeJong poisoned the refreshing hot brew, tea of course, watched by a ghost orangutan, the one he shot and me, so when his men fell backwards, forwards or sideways, he easily dispatched them with a machete, why waste bullets, vendors get suspicious seeing you alone buying bullets.

He imagined he was a butcher, so had no qualms in what he was doing. When he left, a following vampire bat landed and licked up blood, gorged, so heavy could not fly to safety, see, ants were marching to their militant songs to eat up this lot, so was a leopard and a tiger behind them.

"Where are your men?" The vendors would ask Roger too.

The ape had returned, so we saw the spirits come out of the new dead, saw them go through a tunnel of darkness, they were thieves, murderers, drug dealers, pimps, ask yourself, 'Can they get into The Light?' A handful sprinted, sorry drifted into the jungle to add their wailing to jungle sounds.

Roger DeJong was a man possessed with Ramapithecus and fame, soon his clear evil logic did get cloudy with dreams of a cozy future, his undoing.

A pity he did not get the bones and leave Borneo for good, his men had family, cousins with fingers missing, interested parties disfigured by burns, WIVES needing maintained, girlfriends about to look for new boyfriends, all noticed Roger DeJong back alone, that meant he did not want his men to cash in on what he found, never mind, they did cash in for them, cheese wire again?

As Roger was leaving the Hotel Seafront, he noticed rickshaws parked outside, more than usual for the number of hotel guests that used them. The stray Chow dogs were happy, they had lots of wheels to pee on. As the men tried to scare the dogs away, Roger made his break.

Cautiously, Roger entered a side ally hand in pocket, comfort from his handgun, he was heading for any steamer sailing tonight; hundreds of yellow eyes watched him from the beaches, sea crocodiles, ten-foot dark shadows sailed towards him, yet he was not in the sea, bull sharks?

Behind Roger men in Black Hooded smocks followed, them that wanted to know why he killed their friends, twelve of them, most martial art fans, they trusted their fists, the other six held long chopping knives, all had no qualms about using what they had on Roger DeJong. A handful were sobbing so the deceased could see them grieving, lying villains, was for show and give reason to the murder about to be committed.

Likes attract likes, and I thought I was evil not going straight to The Light and Life on a cloud?

A vampire bat watched, flew with them, it was hungry, it would get one of them while he slept, not the same bat at the camp, the ants got it, it was so gorged could not fly.

That orangutan came out of The Light and sat quietly beside me, watching, I looked at it, it grinned back, "Ook," so we followed, no time for argument, these people were responsible for our deaths. I held the ape's left or right hand to help steady it as it flew, I needed steadied too, flying was new.

"Ook," the ape was getting the wrong idea, no more hand clasping.

Suddenly it ate a mango and spat the stone out, then looked at me to wipe its fingers on.

I shook my head, where did it get that mango? How did it get out of The Light? Could I do likewise? Deep down I knew I had not to leave my thread of life in a mess, I had been murdered, had to stay on the Earth to be heard.

"Ook," the ape had been murdered too, that was why she had not stayed in The Light? One thing was for sure, there were other spirits walking next to physicals who never saw them: monkeys, white mice and three blind mice.

"Ook," the ape eating an orchid, where did it get that orchid?

"Ook," the polite reply and was offered a fresh flower.

"No thank you," and smiled, it was a big monkey, best not offend it.

Something else, it understood me, let us hope it understood "No, you ape, me wolf."

"Ook," "never call me monkey again, got it, Ook," the ape warned.

*

1920: As I waited with Steve Jones for the docked steamer to lower gangways, my orangutan joined me, Steve wrinkled his nose for the ghost ape smelled of ape; unwashed fur, toilet, Big Foot, jungle, It pulled a bunch of wild figs from nowhere and ate, I said nothing, it could eat what it wanted, it would never go hungry this side of life; and she never stunk about me; then heard the cobbly wobbles so inches appeared as a gap between us.

"There she is?" Steve excitedly as he had this photograph of his American vet. I peeked a look and then flew to the woman in question, my ape friend took the picture from Steve who thought it a sea breeze and he jumped about to catch it.

He noticed a slug resting on an anchor, then it was gone, slugs get about in Borneo.

"Ook," my ape trying to get my attention scratching her head over Steve, there just was something out of place with this man Steve and was glad she was not a slug.

Steve cleaned his mouth with a handkerchief been in his pocket a week.

Ahead, Steve's help did look pretty, red hair and green eyes and in jungle uniform, shorts, and boots. She smelt good, well, I had been dead a long time so learned I could smell. I was cheating, inspecting the woman without her knowing. Could you imagine her reaction if I were a physical with the ape sniffing my bottom, I did do a tantrum, "Ook," the ape agreeing.

THE UNFAIR ADVANTAGE OF BEING DEAD.

I did not peer through her jungle green uniform to check the color of her lingerie, honest.

"Ook," Calamity peering instead and burst into spirit laughter, at what human women wore. "Ook, did they pooh in them reds, apes were cleaner, she just pooh in those red knickers and have it near all day, yuck, Ook."

"Red smalls, mm, nice," Me so a rotten fig hit me thrown by an ape pretending to be a single she-wolf.

Steve came over, "Miss Lizzy Price?"

She agreed, her soft voice giving instructions to Steve what to do with her luggage, that mountain of boxes over there. This woman was used to giving orders, not my type but Steve seemed fascinated. She was 1) female 2) co-worker 3) petite 4) nicely put together. 5) In close promiscuity, he had fallen in love, the Burke.

"She wears red," I whispered to him to put Calamity off the scent, thinking I was interested in Lizzy Price for Steve.

"You must be hot and sweaty, better change out of the reds," Steve as an unchewed slug antennae with an eye on it looked out of his mouth.

Lizzy Price chinned him, she could forgive his remarks on her underwear, the man had been out here too long, malaria, yellow fever, loneliness, solitary confinement in a tent all taking a toil, but eating a snail, a slug, whatever was at the other end of that antennae was a chinning offence.

"Ook," the ape liked her strawberry deodorant reminding her of food, she knew what strawberries were, rich folk ate them at the Seafront Hotel.

"Calamity"? The ape was a female and needed a name; I threw an invisible banana skin at her, through her and into the sea. This ape was always eating, I did have to sit down with her and find out why? Then offered the woman Lizzy a hand to shake, withdrew and did a raspberry, it was me who was here too long in the jungle without a woman so, was nervous and child-ishly idiotic. Calamity agreed and silently kissed the woman on a cheek, and she felt it for looked about for us.

A white pelican with yellow face colorings about the eyes landed near, expecting food as locals threw them pieces of fish, superstition said good luck too, especially with those remaining sea crocodiles further up the estuary.

The woman Lizzy took out a bitten sandwich from a tartan shoulder bag, checked for plastic, then tossed it to the bird.

"I do that to," Steve amazed.

So did I when I was physical, "What do you think Calamity," the ape looked at her expecting a sandwich, and when it never materialized, "Ook, Ook, Ook," so I thought of a peach cucumber sandwich and gave Calamity it.

Calamity gave me a big ape grin, orangutans have large faces, then ate the sandwich. For all Calamity ate, I was grateful it never passed any waste, and did not think that in case Calamity picked up the thought and just to be the prankish ape, do it, a number two spirit.

We started listening in on their private conversation, another advantage of being dead.

Steve was yapping about butterflies, Lizzy could have ended the one-way chat with, "Oh, I forgot my lipstick back in my cabin, better go get it?" But she listened, part of her brain auditing what she might need, for she was checking her environment and the man in front of her she was to work with.

Noticed ants running about the quay, cages full of pigs, chickens, food stalls, people buying and selling, hustle and bustle, just like home.

How did I know this, I was eavesdropping her mind, another advantage the dead have over the living, how do you think teacup readers make a living? Her mind was tidy, under control, no engagements back home, well I was getting interested myself, anyway Steve did have to know.

"Are you married Lizzy?" Steve.

Yes, that is my Steve, straight to the point.

"You can find out," she replied grinning, her zoo, and museums back home were littered with Steve types, imitations of Harrison Ford. Steve did have to produce something new, his dance along jungle pathways did win her.

"Ook," Calamity added grinning.

"What is that smell, it reminds me of," and Lizzy paused then, "the chimp house."

I looked at Calamity, she grinned and wrapped a furry arm about Lizzy.

"Oh, the smell is on me, oh, so cold to, I feel, possessed," Lizzy, now for a scientist to use those words blew my spirit mind.

"Ook," Calamity unwrapping herself sheepishly from Lizzy.

I could like this girl; she could begin to see me and the ape? Come on Calamity, let us catch up, which was easy, we just floated after them heading for the Sea Front Hotel of course.

On the way Steve ate four more slugs.

Lizzy Price made sure he walked in front, the man was certifiable, an axe murderer, no, he talked nonstop about butterflies? He must wear butterfly printed shorts, and she laughed, and she was spot on, he did.

*

Did I even go to The Light? Yes, I did, the ape took me.

A hole opened in what I know as The Ether, the space between things in space, and before I knew what happened I was grabbed by a hairy hand, and pulled in.

"Ook," filled my ears.

Inside were spirits, apes, monkeys, gorillas, fruit trees, water, everything an orangutan needed to be happy.

"Your family is over there," it was an authoritarian voice, so I looked, and yes, I started recognizing my folk, and they started becoming younger. "Go to them" the voice told me.

I did not want to, I had unfinished business on Earth.

A baby spirit chimp ran to me, an orphan.

In an instant I saw what it saw before murdered for meat. Pain filled me, "It has a family here, its mother is due, she too will be murdered for meat," the voice.

The orangutan took a hand and jumped back through the portal. I was back on Earth with a grinning ape as company. She offered me a melon, I took it, we ate together, "Ook," we were friends.

I looked about for other primates, none, just humans.

"Ook," the ape.

"I shall call you Calamity as you are?"

[CHAPTER 2] — DE JONG'S LUCK

Ghost Romance

De Jong's Luck

Figure 2 Borneo crocodile was saltwater type.

Roger DeJong from one side alley to another went till he reached the docks. Knew he was hunted, needed a steamer? It did have to have an honest crew to stop his hunters who did follow; besides, he wanted his Ramapithecus, he was going to get the fossil ape.

He made a show of himself buying a ticket for a steamer, yes, his ex-friends saw him, not me and the ape, Calamity snarled, she wanted to bite Roger, she wished him on our side in chunks. Clumps of soil, rotten fruit, and annoyed snakes she threw at him, all spirits so he was unscathed, her too.

Then Roger De Jong was gone, he had scrambled roping hanging down the quay. We only knew he was doing this when he screamed, he had grabbed a slither's tail in the dim light and not the rope. That made him fall quick as he let go, lot of slithers in Borneo.

"Ook," Calamity alarmed he had vanished.

"We are ghosts, come on girl," and drifted to where he was last.

"Hiss," the snake making off its tail throbbing.

"Ook," Calamity and vanished, now because she thought of him, she went to him.

I thought of her so went to her, that was one smart monkey.

"Ook," I mean ape, "Ook," all right, Great Ape. Calamity had touchy feelings when called 'MONKEY.'

DeJong was making his way across wet timbers covered in slime, barnacles, and small scuttling crabs. He cursed the cuts on his hands, he knew disease lurked on them know, he reached in a side pocket, out came silver flask, "gurgling" sounds, and with a shake of the head pored the whiskey onto his cuts.

Yeh, he gritted those teeth of his, teeth with gold fillings, the whiskey burned. Whiskey spillage found a pool where a hermit crab lived, a drunk hermit crab lived.

The bloated carcass of something was in the water, Bull Sharks were eating it. I had to stop myself wishing DeJong falling in, I just was not a killer, he was after all kindred in spirit, although a physical.

"Ook," I looked at Calamity who grinned back, she had no qualms about him falling in.

It was his followers coming that made the noise, they met the slither that danced amongst their feet, two were bit, two more fell in amongst the sharks. Even Roger DeJong heard, they screamed loud, extras paid to shout, making Roger hurry heading for river boats laden with produce, to sell, carvings, dried small heads you held by the pigtail, that sort of thingamabobs, even rattan cages with roaches inside for sale, word about Steve even reached the interior, money was to be made with the Europeans, maybe eating roaches was a new fashionable fab. Even the Dayaks tried frying them, with a bit of lemon grass and coconut oil was palatable, delicious.

Anyway, Roger's pursuers created energy, Calamity used it to show her face.

Not that sweet grin reserved for me but gigantic incisors. Just imagine you are trying not to slip on wet timber wrapped in brown seaweed. Then transparent Calamity appears, you scream, cut, and bruise yourself on disease-ridden timbers, just rubbing gangrene in, and slip into the sea where untreated sewage waits, cholera by cupful, then bull sharks get you, bye.

Those that fell, pulled others as they frantically tried not to fall, well needed to hold something?

"You are not family, let go of me," heard often as friendships ended, as grasping hands where slashed with machetes to prove the point. Wrist jewelry taken by the slasher just as the owner fell.

The screams were loud, enough to bring folk to the quay peering. Nothing to help these men done; the steamer lay alongside the dock. Water and human waste shot from holes in the ships side, adding to the sludge on the timber and hitting surviving bad men. Anger built up, they pushed aside comrades too close, three fell in, the others chased Roger DeJong covered in smelly thingmabobs.

"This is your fault," they shouted wiping dirty fingers-on clean hands just holding dry timber, as below sharks circled.

Roger giggled, he thought it funny they loved him so much to die for him, because he was winning his FREEDOM.

In a river boat flashing money, he was off to my camp? How do I know, I am a ghost and learning from my ape, thought of him, so was with him, and orbed his mind? A right nasty place full of dark spirit advisers and a shopping list of goodies to buy in Europe.

"Ook," Calamity joining me, together we settled down in the bow sucking the night jungle energies, we could do with relaxation, we get tired to. Calamity threw a hairy arm across me and invited me closer with steamy eyes.

"Me wolf, you monkey, no," I replied orbing away; she went insane and orbed into a man who screaming holding his head, fell over. I felt murderous, but one more down.

"Ook, Ook," Calamity kissing me with biggest lips ever, "Ook," yes, she was my ape and licked again, then shyly held my left hand, blushing, we had just met.

Spirit fleas jumped off her onto me.

I started scratching, "Hey, I am a ghost, get off me," as I remembered I have no blood and their biting a memory, so did not need coal soap on the bites, I was dead, what a relief.

"YES DEAD, so come to The Light," it was a still voice, not quiet, it was that angelic superior being again come to take me HOME, to watch Life Replays?

"Na," I replied.

*

I was ogling the new vet; confident not seen. She looked what I had wanted a hundred years past, a woman.

Lizzy Price was giving orders to Steve, he had told her about my camp of a hundred years earlier. See, ghosts have big mouths at times, I was bragging, showing off and genuinely wanted him to have a look around, Ramapithecus was here. I liked him, he deserved the house and family I never got and psychiatric help to get off the insect habit.

She was in a Godown checking her jungle equipment, tent, mosquito netting, anti-venom, fly squatter, calamine lotion, diarrhea medicine, those things needed. Alone from Steve she went through her clothing; now I felt I should go, but I did not. I joined a spider and imaged myself onto it, perfect disguise.

It was shady, an overhead light burned, not one hundred watts, a long pull-on switch hung from it. A lonely wolf spider crawled along it, then sailed the rest of the way down. Fortunately, Lizzy never noticed, people fear spiders, 'Horror Films' to blame or an ancestral trait?

"Ook," Calamity trying to eat the spider. The insect reacted to her going on hind legs.

"What was that?" Lizzy heard the ape, she turned to look for a monkey and made monkey sounds hoping to attract a playful Rhesus macaques monkey. Instead, she got an angry orangutan, never call one a monkey.

"Ook," Calamity on the loud side, nesting pigeons flew away. A Black and Crimson Pitta bird was so curious, watched.

"Oh dear, you are an orangutan," Lizzy seeing Calamity who calmed down now; the woman saw Calamity, a ghost. I edged away from the spider nest fearing she did see me.

Watching from a rafter I MADE APE SOUNDS, WHY NOT JUST say hello? Well, she was pretty, so made me senseless. I had no brain so had a legitimate excuse. I was guilty of telling Steve about her red pants, I had to hide.

"Another one," and she looked about.

"Ook," Calamity drifting up to me, Lizzy allowed her gaze to follow. * "A shadow man," alarmed, stuffing colored lingerie places, and even I know what shadow men are as am dead. {The Black and Crimson Pitta bird picked up Lizzy's alarm and flew. The wolf spider jumped at it, fangs dripping venom, it was hungry, baby birds were in a nearby nest. The spider missed as the mother bird was fast. The spider on a silk thread landed on the ground. Lizzy saw it, she did not like spiders behind glass jars, so with her jungle hat she encouraged it away towards the massive Godown open doors. The baby birds were safe for now, an Ornate Brown Snake two meters slithered outside, it could not find a way into the Godown considering how big the doors were, just as well it was short-sighted.?}

*(Now Shadow Folk, dark entities belonging to neither Light nor Earth, who pop their heads from corners to look, repeatedly annoy-

ing the living.)

"No, no, it is me," whose me, foolish ghost I am showing myself? I grinned so she was not sure if I was human or ape as my energy not stable, a reflection on the state of my mind, there was a woman in front of me, a woman, what was I supposed to do?

Lizzy Price stood her ground, taking a good look, then nodded her head, Lizzy was a gifted woman, could differentiate between spirits just as Saint Paul said was one of gifts from Heaven. She did not seem impressed with me as I was with her. Who can blame her, I was up on a rafter looking transparent with an orangutan as company, the later giving Lizzy the impression I must be safe to hang out with as the ape did, or insane, she was deciding to run when "Ook," Calamity drifted to her and held her right hand, gently? Lizzy smiled, in an instant I deducted she liked animals, if Lizzy could like Calamity, could like me, both me and the ape were spirits, so I drifted to stand beside my **good friend** Calamity.

"Ook," Calamity taking my hand and hers and joining us, 'The Three Musketeers.'

Lizzy did not pull her hand away as though the ape spirit might take offence I think, she also had a good look at me. I straightened, looked taller than I was, puffed out my chest, greased my hair, exhaled a cod piece, cleared my throat; she greeted all with hilarious laughter, I was harmless, even though I had been sneakily watching her.

I felt her body heat from her thought, which made me think I was not to be alone anymore.

"Firstly, no, stay alone Buddy, and secondly tell me your name." I was just another Steve to order about. Worse she had read my thoughts; my amorous intentions, my career as a ghost leerer had just ended.

"I am Henry Adamson, a murder victim, and my friend Calamity here, he murdered her also, shot her right between the eyes. I spoke to her directly the mind.

"Ook, Calamity agreeing, falling dead and rolling over with her tongue out, eyes X.

"Must have been long ago," Lizzy sensing our old energies, and my boots were not fashionable, my clothes not designer labelled, I was an antique, an umbrella stand, clothed.

"My grave, is in the old European cemetery, not cared for, weeds as high as the crumbling gravestones, rats live there and that means snakes.

R.I.P. the cemetery is because of that, but interesting people there? Hans the railway manager for one, never built the railway, died of rabies.

Elizabeth Warburton, wife of Captain Fokker? All died early of disease and warfare, why they came in the first place? Willie Duff, he was a pirate, imitated Captain Kid right to the hangman, want to visit?" I asked.

After a pause, "Alright, show me," Lizzy thinking she could learn more from a headstone than a glowing ghost, the ape glowed too, and Lizzy was a bit of tease, so twirled and her bottom glided together, and she headed for the big Godown doors. Me, I was cement poured, unable to cope with a woman's anatomy so close.

"Ook," an excited ape.

"Impressive," a foolish ghost hoping for more twirls, ah come on, I was lonely, give me a break, she was a woman in jungle uniform green shorts. Not standard jungle issue as seemed short all right and tight, inviting sweat rashes, redness, itching and people sure you caught a strange variety of S.T.D. and making sure everyone knew, you were contagious.

She waited for our two orbs to pass and followed.

"Hello Steve," she said stopping.

We waited, she did not explain where she was going, she was

a vet, her spiritual gifts she hid.

The Ornate Brown Snake did not wait, those Godown doors were open sixteen feet plus, only we spirit saw its energy slither in.

The mother Black Crimson Bird saw and flew about popping on the snake, her babies were vulnerable.

The snake was hungry, so was the Mongoose that ran after it, a battle of life and death ensured, who did win, snake or mammal.

The mother bird sat on her young watching.

"Are you going to Henry Adamson's grave?" Steve asked, "He is my friend," without thinking I put, the words in his mind, blame Lizzy's contagious excitement.

"Friend?" She asked as I was dead but got no reply so decided Steve was weird and be kept at a distance. She also decided he been eavesdropping at the door to know where we were going, he needed replaced, Lizzy felt uncomfortable in his presence now. To confirm her fear, she was sure he just put a roach in his mouth, his mouth moved, she looked away, then back, his mouth had moved again.

On the way to the grave and at the grave, Steve told Lizzy about me and Calamity. I thrilled hearing about my exploits as an explorer, Steve had an imagination, having me cut my way through jungles filled with SNAKES, escaping head-hunters and pirates, sending extinct fossils back to European universities, I had a name then, and there are wall pictures of Henry in the Seafront Hotel.

A captivated Lizzy Price looked at my orb, she also watched Steve, making sure a safe distance separated them.

I grinned widely, I knew she was liking me, a ghostly advantage.

"Ook," Calamity understanding that look so was a jealous ape so, chatting ape gibberish in Steve's mind nonstop like a woman can, causing Steve to jump about as if covered in ants, and I want a woman, was I insane?

Lizzy gave Steve an understanding look, been in the jungle too long, she understood, he needed a slug.

Lizzy smiled and thought figs, Calamity cheered, Steve felt left out, he sensed us, but he mentally blocked us out; his scientific mind subconsciously rejected us, more like terrified of ghosts.

But he had Lizzy all to himself as we walked to the cemetery for, we needed our energy to orb.

"Spooky?" Lizzy summed up the overgrown cemetery noticing the tall grass moving hating being alone with Steve, ready at an instant to karate chop his neck if he put a hand on her.

"Too early for rats, snake probably," Steve unfolding a piece of metal with a fork at the end.

They kept to the path, away from the edges where snakes lurked, waiting for a running rodent on the path, easy meals. But not today, myself and Calamity warned them six times of danger, six times Steve became a hero with his stick, encouraging the reptiles to shift.

Lizzy was impressed, Steve might seem funny, but he knew snakes, so did she, she was a vet. Then again jungle explorers took risks with snakes when they stepped into the creepers. But being a beautiful woman, Lizzy knew men tried it on, knew Steve was doing exactly that, he did not need well fitted clothes, or manicured haircuts, a new car, cash, being handsome to be noticed. He was plainly excited; he was like a teenager told to show the new girl about school.

"He is my friend," I told her.

"Ook," Calamity adding.

Lizzy knew she did have to guard her thoughts with us

about, "Not out to hurt him," she replied to us two.

"Ook," Calamity looking at Steve, he was clearly smitten. I felt Lizzy's energy field, it was red, Lizzy was a strong-willed person wanting new horizons, Steve better watch out, as a spirit could see his orange energy, he was sensitive and would be hurt with Lizzy, Steve was afraid of girls dropping him, and now he was blindly walking where millions had trodden before, the dump yard.

There was my headstone, 'HENRY ADAMSON, EXPLORER, SHETLAND, MURDERED 1905.'

"What were you looking for?" Lizzy aloud.

"Fossils," Steve wanting to keep the conversation on a physical level with him involved, "he found Ramapithecus bones and," repeated the stories beginning. Lizzy was impressed, Steve had taken so long describing Peter Pan and Captain Hook all the snakes he cleared were back, on the path waiting for him. Oh heck, we have to leave by the back door," which took us to a small rusty swing gate, down through graves to an exit at the back onto a proper tarmac sticky road, the road tar reacting to the heat, why lots of flying insects wiggled on the tar surface and birds waited for us to clear off. One a Crimson Pitta bird who had hungry babies.

But we did stop on the other side of the exit gate, "These graves are not hallowed, badmen and women here," Steve not liking the coldness about him. Hairs on his exposed limbs became erect, why he even left the slugs alone.

"My murderer," I pointed out to Lizzy.

She stopped and read, "Roger DeJong, 1905," all it said, and he was lucky he got that, most had no names.

"Come on, I can tell you away from these graves," Steve outside on the road, safe from the slithers. Lizzy walked on, she felt she had stepped back in time. I was no longer just a floating specter, I now had a body, all right, skeleton, but it was physical, she now could picture me looking for fossils and ignored the murder scene, it was lunch time.

Menu, Hinava, grilled spiced mackerel, with watermelon to cool down, but I could not eat, I was dead, "Ook," Calamity wanting figs and honeycomb, "Ook," complaining she was dead too.

The couple sat on a white tiled floored restaurant with an overhead fan. A singing Dollarbird in a cage. Calamity and I were up at the spinning fan, resting absorbing electricity, THINKING OF WAYS TO FREE THE bird.

"I can buy it," Lizzy's thoughts interrupted ours, "Ook," Calamity, happy she could read our minds. Myself, panicky, she must know I had admired more than her strong spirit?

But Lizzy, the restauranter told her songbirds are pricey, jungles cleared of them, soon just be leaf ants and tree snakes in trees.

The bamboo cage door opened, and the Dollar bird hoped out, away it went happy it had met me and Calamity who freed it.

Lizzy did not explain to Steve inside the restaurant what happened, the staff might twig from his excitement they had something to do with the bird's escape.

When the waiters returned Lizzy and Steve were finishing off their puddings, Kuih Lapis, sweet goey rice flour puddings. The owner looked at Lizzy, he was trying to connect Lizzy wanting to buy the bird and its sudden flight to freedom.

I entered his mind, "hello," I said, "Ook," Calamity copied.

The man screamed and ran off, he did be better watching his step than trying to get us two out of his head, a big cobra seen eating a rat close by.

Outside and at a safe distance, Lizzy told Steve what we had done, he was impressed, "I could not have done better," he replied, did I detect a hint of jealousy? No but Lizzy did, she had seen friends turn sour over ownerahip of her.

Nobody owned Lizzy Price.

In a flash Steve stuffed a roach in his mouth, insect legs wiggled from his lips.

Lizzy stared at Steve's lips, Steve returned her gaze with a giant smile and the roach escaped.

He tried forcing himself not to give chase.

Now as they made their way to the docks, for Lizzy wanted the price of a river boat to go upstream to my camp, and a mental check list of food, mosquito netting, anti-venom, camping utilities, stove and lighters, matches were out, jungle rained every day.

"Did Roger DeJong get the bones?" Lizzy asked Steve watching Dayak men in tribal outfits posing for European camera tourists.

"Not sure, my friend on the other side, please do not think I am crazy, Henry is dead, but he enters my head and chats, and gives me the impression the bones are still at the campsite, seems Roger DeJong got his chips before he could tell his rotten friends where he hid them," Steve.

"Well, we will find them, and you are not crazy, I have already met Henry, I am sure he can find them and tell me," Lizzy. Steve was aghast, went a shade of pale, his flame was chatting with me?

Lizzy had become the object of his devotion; Troy destroyed over a rejected love. I felt his mental alarm, I was a ghost, what could he fear from me? Lizzy replied for him, "You look at lingerie."

"Ook," Calamity answered, I had reason to fear, Lizzy was mediumistic, "Ook," and I shook my spirit head, I sure was as a ghost attracted to Lizzy, but I was dead. "Ook," meaning 'I am dead and available.'

Then Steve grabbed Lizzy's hand, right or left, a hand belonging to Lizzy, he was excited, he could not take his ogling eyes of her breasts, all he wanted to do was tell her about a cool restaurant they could go for foods, but her 'lovely melons to grab' escaped his mouth instead of 'lovely honey melons to eat there.'

Lizzy chinned him, that made twice in the story already.

Chinned folk might count sheep, stars, fast cars to fast to count, melons even, but our Steve counted roaches spinning around his head.

*

Lizzy tucked into her Char Siew Fan, tangy roast pork as Steve ate melon balls, trying hard to keep to his vegetarian diet. He was afraid she might see him as weak if he ate meat. Frankly, Lizzy could not care as cared not for Steve except for the distance between them. Often, he scraped his chair closer, often Lizzy scraped her chair away, my, they were going round the table in circles. Steve was heading for a chinning, were his luck ran out and needed a dentist to tidy up the broken teeth, but they would match his shiners?

"So, DeJong escaped to Europe thinking he was safe to return someday and get the bones?" Lizzy.

"That was his idea, why he killed Henry, Ramapithecus would make him famous, wealthy. His local friends here, Roger came back thinking his friend's dead or not bothered any more.

Enough to drop the De from his name, grow a beard and ditch his blond hair to black, blending in with the locals.

But his movements came to the notice of the triad he had been involved with, only Roger DeJong would want to go to Henry Adamson's camp.

So, when he went upriver in his river boat, another followed, when he expected his boat to stay, it went away, another boat pulled up, ten men rushed the quay, pelicans flew off, Toucans complained, fruit bats filled the sky, but they exhausted themselves for nothing, Roger was ten miles further inland digging up Ramapithecus.

Dayak head-hunters also watched him, the ten badmen were about a mile away when the Dayaks jumped Roger DeJong.

Never had a chance to shoot, they used a blow pipe, full of tranquilizers, Roger swooned, unconscious.

When the ten badmen arrived, Roger was gone, the places where he had been digging were there, a handful stood guard, others started digging, rotted canvas bags uncovered, joy and jubilation filled the badmen, so did greed.

Now five men agreed amongst themselves there were too many to share the rewards of selling fossil bones. They talked in whispers, and the other five over there talked in whispers, agreeing amongst themselves there were too many shareholders.

Now five men lay dead, hacked with machetes, but the smiles on the living did not last long.

"Rprt," was the sound of a blow pipe, again "Rprt," and five badmen swooned.

The Dayak head-hunters appeared, Roger swung from under a pole, these five men joined him. They swore at Roger blaming him for their predicament.

One of the original badmen who had been set upon by his friends was still alive.

He pleaded in Cantonese for mercy, they took his head, they did shrink it later, took all the heads, they did sell them to tourists in Sandakan. The headless corpses were better than a "TRESPASSING," notice.

They did be skeletons soon; ants scented dinner and were hurrying back to nests with the news.

A brave Wolf Spiders waited on the appendage of the murder scene, they did pick off lone ants, careful not to become an ant dinner themselves.

A giant foot long purple and yellow centipede hurried in the opposite direction; she did not want to be eaten by thousands of ants.

The Dayak people went away, they did not want ants running over their feet making them foolishly jump here and there.

"About twenty minutes later Roger and his old pals woke swinging from their poled positions.

He tried what the remaining badmen had, cash for freedom.

The Dayaks took their cash, what did the Dayaks want with cash, guns, too noisy for jungle warfare, Clothes, they did not wear, headdress, the birds provided, women, they had their own, but steel machetes, yes from traders?

Roger grew hoarse and quietened, he watched leaf cutter ants carrying leaves, wiggly worms, birds had dropped at the approach of the men, looked at the toe imprints on the feet impressions of his captors, he had lots to keep his mind off his fate.

It was when they crossed surging powerful streams that Roger knew he was dead, they could not care if he drowned, and six times he did. Under the water he saw small fish and angry water snakes they disturbed fishing, one bit him; JUNGLE REVENGE it was.

What goes round comes round, the Dayaks noted, they did make sure the venom killed him, the snake was avenging a murder Roger had committed.

A relative of the Kingfisher family waited also for them to clear off, the snake was small, much more filling than tiny fish that required a dozen dives to fill a tummy.

Roger DeJong began seeing his life playout, he was proud of his successes and cursed himself for his failures in crime, he was not repentant, not a 'sorry' chirped, grunted, barked, or squeaked his lips. Oh, he was remorseful he had not gotten Ramapithecus, and cursed whoever would find them.

Well pretty soon they came to a large clearing with long houses; excited villagers saw what the men had brought home.

Where they cannibals also, this was not Melanesia, but Borneo?

[CHAPTER 3] — PETER

Figure 3 original 1920 photo of mosquito, Sandakan, Borneo.

"This story is fascinating," Lizzy hooked, Steve smiled, that meant she did be given him all the attention while it lasted. He hoped he remembered to put on after shave, then remembered he never wore any. He put both his hands over his mouth and felt for insect parts, finding none, confidence to manage Lizzy filled him.

"Ook," Calamity doing hand movements that explained with a sniff snort why he was a loner, he stunk; then Calamity violently waved her hand ridding it of spirit boogies, which splatted onto Steve, although he could see them, he felt them.

Panic gripped him, dinner had escaped, a roach or millipede?

Cursing he sipped his coffee, aware now that coffee breath was as bad as garlic essence unaware something spiritual sank to the cup's bottom; Calamity giggled. I almost said, "Stupid monkey," and because thought it she picked it up.

I took a minute break as an ape went and tied me in ecto-plasm knots.

Steve smelled his oxers, his socks, he had sandals on, not a relief as all needed washed, his unmentionables, yes, he would change them daily now, just in case. Youth, it was too late, the smell of pee was strong and a troop of passing monkeys blamed.

"Ook," Calamity laughing as she read his fears and why? "Ook," agreeing he should change his unmentionables daily, again wafting away spirit flies attracted by delicious essences.

"Look Steve, you did think you had never seen a woman be-fore?" I put these thoughts into his mind. As Lizzy waved away spirit flies, remarkably interesting she saw ghost flies?

Steve angered and Lizzy noticed his cheeks flush, so guess-ing a conversation was going on, joined in.

She felt his answer to my line of questioning, I was correct, Steve living in jungles too long and become a recluse, loner, un-able to chat to females in local Starbucks, "I lack city clothes, I am broke, I have no driving license, who wants me?" Extremely dangerous thoughts, apart from inviting Calamity, he was open-ing himself up to other spirits that would twist his mind into another Roger De Jong, and to overcome, he must forget girls, butterflies were harmless and safer.

Lizzy withdrew, she felt she had entered a private no-go area, and at same time was glad, now she understood Steve, be careful not to drive him back into the jungle.

"Steve, she is your co-worker, business and romance never mix, trust me?" I mooted in his mind.

"Ook," Calamity agreeing, looking at me ogling, just never gives up.

"Yeh, well she can see you, chat with you private, the great explorer Henry Adamson, who knows what you are talking about?" Steve thought back becoming agitated over coffee table memories.

"Ook," Calamity enveloping him in a comforting freezing mist.

"B***** off monkey," and Calamity hurt, immediately Steve wished he had never said what he did and slumped ashamed. Never call an ape a monkey twice in a day, with agility she rushed him and messed up his hair and mind, so a blank stare possessed him.

"Let us get back to our expedition, hello Steve, are you home?" Lizzy asked.

Slowly his eyes demisted focusing on her chest, was obvious the way color came back to him and why.

Lizzy pulled her shirt closed and clicked fingers under Steve's nose. A tiny mite answered her from the right nostril.

Lizzy was horrified, what was Steve?

Since we were all preoccupied, never noticed the smartly dressed Eurasian youth enter and order coffee. The clothes taken out of a sea chest from last century, they had a moth ball smell about them.

Unlike Steve he wore crocodile leathers with white toe caps, polished to shine by the shoeshine boy outside.

His pink shirt ironed, now crumpled in the sleeves as rolled to the elbows.

A gold Rolex watch adorned his left wrist, it worked, were as Steve's cheap watch died in a jungle stream, so was ornamental only, with Donald Duck still smiling from the watch face.

Peter got up and sat next to Lizzy and Steve, he was direct, "Word has it you are going upriver.

Peter's good looks startled Lizzy, for a moment she was off guard and should have asked, "We just got here, how did you find out?"

Steve noticed the Eurasian was more handsome than himself, which was easy, so huffed again, when he should have said, "Na mate, someone been filling your lugs with wax," in a broad imitated Aussie ascent and pretended a Foster's Beer was under his seat, see, no one in their right mind offended a drunk Aussie butterfly collector.

All knew about Crocodile Dundee and Steve Irwin, and about this insect eating Lonnie Tune here not to offend.

"I am Peter and work as a plantation manager upriver, I will be going there soon, I can give you a lift to where?" Peter smiling, and summoned the non-Muslim server over, "Another round of Kopitiam," Peter drinking European Americano Coffee to show he was native. The waiter brought back condensed milk, the punctured tin, and a list of fruit cordials to mix with it.

Steve forgot about insects, his lips trembled, licked by a tongue, condensed milk he loved.

Peter also ordered Ondeh, sweet potato cake balls coated in coconut and melted brown sugar in the middle, white paper napkins placed at everyone's side, the brown sugar always exploded OUT.

Peter ordered other cakes; he wanted his victims here, not out there away from his scheming mind for he was a schemer dreamer.

Beautiful singing came from caged Black-browed Babblers, almost extinct, a warm breeze blew in open windows, the sir smelt of spices, street vendors were frying onions and curry powders. Lizzy felt her tummy wanted filled; her mind wanted to know why Peter had chosen them? Try as she might concentrate her mind mediumistically into his, he blocked her; he was good.

Peter was no weakling, determined, muscular from Kung Fu training, single minded so when he set out to get what he wanted, he got it, no side tracking, was he a good or bad soul?

A faded wall poster of 'The Good, The Bad, The Ugly, Western' was on the café' wall.

A Chinese fiddler played soulful music as entertainment, backed up by a rhesus monkey on a chain with waist coat and top hat. Calamity orbed above wanting to free, yes, a monkey.

Lizzy took her attention from Peter to the monkey, she would ask to buy it, then set it free.

Peter followed her gaze, he nodded, he liked her sympathy, kindness, weakness he could use to win the game started a hundred years ago.

Peter went over to the fiddler, they chatted, the man knew who Peter was, he could have the monkey, and thanked him for the cash to buy another, yes, a depleted songbird would be better accompaniment to his sad music.

Lizzy was amazed, Steve was dumfounded, now he had this handsome Eurasian as well as Henry to contend with for Lizzy's affection.

Steve needed to sit by himself and think, he had just met Lizzy, she might be an ogre, her inner temperament Medusa, but Steve was smitten, she could have horns, which did be fine, he needed help, he needed a roach to chew.

Outside Lizzy could not thank Peter enough for the monkey.

"We must go to the edge of Sandakan town limits, where the jungle is, then let it go, if it wants freedom, remember it has been caged, dependent on a human for food and safety.

"Well, we are going upriver as you know, we can free it at camp site, if it comes back?"

"I will take it, he can roam about my garden with my mongoose," Peter smiling assuring Lizzy the monkey did be safe.

Steve made childish mental faces behind Peter's back.

Lizzy noted, she did sleep with a revolver on boat, then remembered Henry and Calamity did protect her, and smiled and thoughts are alive, so an ape and ghost picked them up and smiled too.

Steve was not smiling and in the melee of people, watchers, noting strengths and weaknesses.

Then I and Calamity arrived, the red aurora about Peter warned us he was strong, his mind closed, that was strange, was he expecting us, how did he know to do this and why were his thoughts so private?

"Ook," Calamity liking the looks of the man, "Silly ape, looks could hide a monster;" Calamity forgave me as called her, 'ape,' and "Ook," such a good-looking man must be an angle.

I joined Steve to join his dumbfound mood, "You, go away," was his line to me as I might take Lizzy away, "How, I am dead fool," I shouted back and left his mind.

Lizzy might be dominant, but so was Peter, he showed her his river boat, nice little cabin at the back, boat full of modern cargo, mobile phones, game consoles; destined for Dayaks and other in-land tribal people.

Peter portrayed himself as a trader, a speaker of dialects, languages as well, one day he did like to go to Europe and see if the outside world was any better than Sandakan? He spoke to tourists at the Seafront Hotel, read about Holland, listened to market gossip before he became Peter, then folk gossiped behind him, afraid of his shadow.

He was an orphan, local Eurasian families took him in, and as soon as he wanted to stand on his own feet, was oaky, 'bye then,' as his adoptive parents were glad, he was going, why?

Who was Peter?

Peter had lore and used lore to make himself who he was, Peter.

And sorry, no surname yet, Peter had introduced himself as 'Peter.'

Would goodness rise in him as attracted to Lizzy? But men were, and did that mean badness rule him? It was a burning ambition to fulfil what his ancestors left him, lore that wrapped about a dream of a house back in the homeland, Holland, which was rich, born and bred locally.

*

Lizzy stood watching laborer's carry her boxes down to his boat, wondering if it were overloaded, she could see the lazy sea crocodiles sunbathing on the flats dreaming of her, as dinner.

"I do not like him," I was inside her mind, "Ook," Calamity disagreeing.

Big mistake as Lizzy thought I was jealous, when I was not, it was the way his mind blocked probing.

"Ook," Calamity going to attach herself to Lizzy, "Ook," an ape raspberry.

I drifted over to a Toucan on a branch over the river. Its heavy large beak rainbow painted. Together we sat watching the boat leave, powerful Yamaha outboard motors at the back pushing it forward, making those lazy crocodiles materialize in the estuary. They were ever hopeful, unwanted produce entered the water, enough to feed them and the sharks so left each other alone.

Lizzy could not stop snapping pictures with her camera, Peter knew she had already taken photos of him in her panoramic landscapers.

He did not accidentally bump the mobile into the murky waters, he did not have a police record either, although the police knew him asking you, 'Peter, are you, his friend?'

"Peter," folk shivered and whispered when he was a good distance from them. No one ever spat red Betel nut onto his footsteps, he had friends everywhere, they did tell him, then a bogie person did visit you, or the uncertainty of a visit drove you mental.

All whipped up by little knowledge on Peter, just that he was wealthy, and you were not?

Steve to be next to Lizzy, came towards her, it was his job to point out the interesting things to photograph.

Poor Steve because the boat lurched to avoid illegal timber floating down, oh no, yes, he did, he bumped her.

"PLOP," the sound of the camera entering the water were flower petals floated by.

Censored as Lizzy tore a strip off Steve, Peter took note, she did not like Steve who could be useful?

What would Lizzy be to Peter, "Look scum, I have a European girlfriend?" No, not even that, Peter was so handsome he had lots of girls, Lizzy he knew might get him his dream to Europe, Holland particularly.

She was now part of his lore, stories fed to him growing up.

Alone in her cabin, "I think this is yours?" It was her camera, I had aported it, what a dive amongst those reptiles, ha, no meal on me tonight?

"Supposed to be waterproof?" Lizzy holding back happiness until the mobile worked, she took a snap of me then went to album.

"Who rescued it?" Peter looking in the cabin as the mosquito curtain opened for air.

I had a look, who was that white mist.

"Please knock next time, and yes it was just taken," Lizzy allowing annoyance to creep into her voice, she did not like men sneaking up on her shoulder. She remembered me hiding with spiders watching her unpack.

Peter noted, he noticed everything down to the fact Steve should change his unmentionables more often; he noticed the white orb too.

"Ok, I just came to tell you dinner is ready, fish noodle soup in milk, and mango fruit, come and eat, come on?" Peter beckoning Lizzy to follow.

I went to, "Ook," Calamity with her nose in the air, she liked Peter, he was a walking David sculpture.

I shook my head in my orb, I looked at Steve, sulking, he noticed my orb, well at last, "You her hero now?"

I felt so sad, went over to him, "Listen buddy, keep your feelings for her wrapped, she might not like you that way," I was inside his head, he shook me out. For effect dug earwax and flicked it where I was.

I followed him to dinner, not that I could eat with them, but I did mentally imagine eating what they ate, Calamity smiled and ate imagined figs, mango and melons and bugs creeping on them as pudding.

Peter took pictures and spent a bit longer studying them, he was looking for me. Why was I so special, I, Henry Adamson too was in the lore Peter was unwrapping on this journey upriver?

*

Daylight, the river boat now tied to the old jetty, which brought back memories, myself and Calamity zoomed away looking for the path to my camp.

"Tear drops falling from my eyes," I sang as Calamity rained spirit tears that hitting the jungle soil, caused giant creepers, jungle squash to grow and red ants dead for a hundred years to resurrect. Believe me and join Steve and his slugs ha, ha.

Later: "This is how Henry described it?" Steve looking about, picking up an old machete, a tattered black shirt hung from a branch, the remains of an old tent stuck out of the soft sand.

Crocodile prints and slither wiggles on the sand, impending danger, Steve ignored and chased a land crab; it had wiggly legs so, must taste delicious.

"Crocodile tracks," Peter pointing near Steve who looked worried and joined the main party.

"What did you mean Henry Adamson?"

Lizzy pretended not to hear, but she was interested, only myself and Steve had told her about me, where did Peter hear of me?

"The explorer, he came this way, just like the street story tellers tell you," Peter, "Yes, they filled my head full of Henry Adamson tales, a city of gold he discovered upriver, all fables my friend, no such city as I trade here abouts," Peter.

Lizzy now regretted blocking me out about warning her, 'I do not like him.'

Well, me and Calamity were zooming back to the main party, we had not reached my campsite ten miles on, but a 'Big Cat,' heading for a drink at the river had. It was a clouded leopard, the party did have to stick together while trekking, any stragglers did be pounced on, bitten, and dragged into the bush.

I told Lizzy, her face lit up, out came the camera, "What have you been told?" Peter. Lizzy stared at him, he stared back, that white mist was guiding HIM to his lifetime dream, a ticket to Holland, the orb belonged to him.

The white mist took on a male handsome face, disarming Lizzy, no one that handsome could be evil.

Lizzy used fingers to tidy herself up.

"She speaks to a ghost," it was Steve full of sour grapes, destroying his chances with Lizzy trying to drive other men away, and ghosts.

Peter nodded, he knew about a jetty, it belonged to Henry Adamson, now he was sure I was helping them to Ramapithecus. He was a believer of The After Life, and sliding towards, 'THIS MAN IS DANGEROUS,' on the scale of human interaction.

Those old ape bones was famous for never hitting the headlines.

Lizzy mentioned she smelt leopard, for a moment Peter was faceless, then laughed, she took him a fool, smell a leopard, from here, that was rich?

Peter went on assembling his men to carry his wares into the jungle, the men up front scything with machetes jungle over the path, behind two stayed with the boat.

The leopard waited, it did drink then follow waiting for stranglers, it was not that hungry to commit suicide. Then there was tonight, humans slept, guards fell asleep, she knew guards were tasty and lasted ages. She hoped the guards here were not old and arthritic but young, juicy, and chewy.

And that is exactly what happened, Peter now making sure not followed, others back in Sandakan were curious why he was burdening himself with Europeans?

Well, the guard was walking feeling big with a semi-automatic rifle, then the Big Cat dropped on him, landed on his head breaking his neck so he crumpled. Peter ordered him back to the jetty and was walking alone, yes, the leopard would drag him up a tree and have three meals a day.

At camp an agitated Peter, his man was missing, question was why? He looked at Roger's lurking nearby mist, the face in it negatively shook. "Go look for me then?" Peter ordered and the face in the orb darkened, then brightened quickly as Lizzy neared. The male ghost here huffed and puffed his stink of decay away, sucking in sweet smelling jungle flower scent as replacement.

Peter shook his head in disgust, "Dead and buried old man, Lizzy is mine," and left the dinner table and got his men to follow him back along the trail, he was expecting town trouble.

"Ook," Calamity drifted after them, she liked handsome men, silly ape.

"For someone whose been dead a century, you are not green and moldy," Lizzy in her mind, was she complimenting me?

I appeared there, I even had time to flatten my hair and take off my Australian bush hat with corks dangling from the rim and spirit flies trapped there vanished helping me out.

I smiled, she was a handsome woman, Judas Priest, her frontage was breathing, it was moving up and down, I just did not know what to say but did know where to look, not try and force conversation.

Lizzy was aware of my ghostly stare, "Been a long time, has it? She asked nodding.

Then it came, "Ook," Calamity showing us the picture in her mind, a leopard eating a man, and another Peter at the docks setting up men to ambush whoever took his man?

In the darkness he had not noticed the fallen semi-automatic rifle or flattened bush from the leopard and man's weight.

An alarmed Lizzy asked, "Why all the rifles, who was Peter, and would he endanger them?"

"He seems awfully interested in our party, I try to figure who he is, but he blocks, think I will rustle through his belongings and find out things?" I spoke to Lizzy.

"Lingerie?" She was naughtily rotten.

"Nope, might be a Fosters," I put on an Aussie drawl avoiding anything connected to sex.

"I have had enough; I am here too?" Steve annoyed he was not in our conversation, so he angrily got up and then was unaccounted for?

Inside Peter's tent I saw his ruck sack that one of the laborer's carried for him, Peter knew cash bought labor.

I sensed the same aura on his personal belongings as on him, it was familiar, where had I sensed before?

"Ook," Calamity joining me, she was not happy, then attacked the personal belongings of Peter, knocking them about. I cringed making my orb smaller, Peter did know someone had been snooping here.

Pulling Calamity away we joined Lizzy looking at photos she had taken, she was studying intently, we drifted into her mind so we could look through her vision.

Peter had an orb usually with him, he must know. I asked Lizzy if she could filter the orbs to see if there was a face in any? Oh, the wonders of technology, there was Roger DeJong. Why should Roger be haunting Peter?

"Peter knows about you Henry?" Lizzy sad that handsome Roger was a rotter.

"Ook," Calamity agreeing now distracted by male orangutan sounds in the trees above.

Now I was alone with Lizzy, we talked about why Roger murdered me, for the bones of Ramapithecus.

"What is Peter's last name?" Lizzy asked, none knew.

Then the mist appeared, frightening us, Lizzy was mentally troubled, doubling up, falling to the ground.

I rushed into her mind, "DeJong," I shouted and pushed him. Lizzy now saw his face, darkness clung to his spirit, he had not favored well in the After Life; well, he was an unrepentant murderer, thief, scoundrel of the worst, and he had lifted Lizzy's plans out of her mind and stopped because I threw him out.

"Ook," Calamity recognizing her killer and attacked.

"Gr," Roger and added "mummy," as knew even in Spirit he was no match for an ape. "Oh, the monkey I killed," then snarled animalistically but was Roger DeJong, this spirit needed help quick before it became so lost it became solid blackness.

"Ook," Calamity chasing his dark orb away.

"I better help my friend," meaning orangutan, Lizzy nodded, she felt ill, drained, sore head, and watched me go, my orb zooming, "I do not get this with Henry," she means headache for she is thinking of romance. "Thank you," she said and added, "Henry," of course I never heard that, but a jealous man did and an ape.

"I think I hate you Henry, hate you all," and faded away, Steve eaten up by covetousness.

Roger found Peter making his way to my old camp, he had left us behind without tent, food, or utilities, out here that was akin to murder?

Peter absorbing Roger turned to face us two so when we reached him, his mental block and Roger's energy stopped our advance.

I decided Peer had to go.

"Ook," calamity agreeing.

Time passed, Peter's party moved, and we did not see Roger come out of the young man, and I concluded Roger was possessing Peter; an exorcism did bring us a kinder Peter.

"The physicals stopped, that was a tigers roar, only the Dayaks and tribal people swore they still roamed Borneo, a tiger spirit or a real tiger?

Then the bush parted so quickly, and a rhino rushed across the path of Peter's entourage, knocking two over; the jungle did not like these men.

"Mm," Peter sounding disgust at the pools of squashed human anatomy as Rhinos are heavy animals with horns, so explains the pieces of whatever hanging from nearby branches.

"Ook," Calamity and became one orb with me, she was trembling, afraid of the jungle, yes, I felt the spirits of animals, plants and murdered people moving about us heading for Peter. A spirit crocodile waded past, followed by six more, Peter back home had made shoes of them, cooked their meat, and sold their skins.

Amid screams of terror Peter pushed on, he had about seven miles to the old camp, in the end he stopped and began Buddhist chants to rid his men of their spirit entourage.

Of these the stronger men stood and chanted also, a couple of the weaker fled into the jungle, pythons waited for them, a meal would keep their bellies full for months.

After a while, things calmed down, Peter looked about him, he had six men left.

"We split equal shares from what I sell here?" Peter told them, there was silence, what would Peter sell, and would he kill them off, greed had entered their rotten thinking. "We should find fossils soon, European museums will buy them, each of you will be millionaires," Peter needed to bolster their courage and loyalty, as for the later, he no longer trusted people he had to share with; he knew as time went on new shareholders did vanish.

The new shareholders trusted Peter up to a point, he was Peter, he lived amongst them, they had no idea he was planning to immigrate to Holland. Roger DeJong was his direct ancestor and influenced him about the wonders of Europe. Peter was better off in Borneo, but affluence had blinded him, in Europe he did visit Monte Carlo and the French Riviera; have a big car, nasty guard dogs and women hanging onto his wealth, and he did treat them accordingly.

Poor Peter needed a local shaman to rid the attachment of Roger, send him back to the dark realms, you see like Lizzy, he was mediumistic.

*

"Ook," Calamity telling me what Lizzy had said, apes in spirit were better at eves dropping than humans.

"Really," and mused over the situation. Could a spirit have a romance with a human physical? Roger attached to Peter so why not me and Lizzy?

"Ook," Calamity excited picturing my romantic future, then went moody., it was with Lizzy.

Quickly I pictured Calamity with us, making sure she understood she was with us.

"I will send you and your ape to hell where you belong," Steve muttered following Peter, why because he thought if he helped that man, in return Peter did help him to rid the world of me, and Calamity. Poor Steve, eaten by jealousy, years of loneliness had affected him, filled with the same dream as I, Roger and Peter suffered from, the dream of success except with a difference, it did have a heated greenhouse not full of flowers, but insects.

No leopard ate Steve or snake bit, or bat sucked heaven knows? We, myself, and the ape only became aware of him as we watched Peter have his remaining men dig, Roger was showing him mentally where to? So, it was not long before wrapping appeared, so old it fell apart, but not the fossils inside.

Peter took a jaw fragment from a man, his eyes drifted away, his men knew he was dreaming cash, they thought Peter crazy, a monkey jaw was only valuable in Chinese medicine.?

Soon Peter had a canvas sack full of Ramapithecus and another filling with extinct animals.

"I am rich," Peter thought.

"I am rich," Roger thought.

"Peter, remember me, I can help you if you help me?" Steve suddenly emerging from the jungle, his legs covered in leeches swollen with his blood.

Men roughed him, waiting for Peter to give the word to kill.

Steve was afraid, he was no longer peach colored but white.

"What can you do for me?" Peter asked, always the businessperson.

"Kill him, he belongs to Henry, skin him for the ants," Roger inside Peter's mind.

"Help you get these fossils out of Borneo, I send specimens back to Europe always," Steve coughed out his own tooth fragments.

Peter thought, skinning him would be fun, his screams heard by those at the jetty, especially Lizzy, making her subdued, he liked that. Peter was bad, what was his name, Peter Jong, his mother had dropped the De, he was a De Jong.

"Ok Steve, you live now, but why desert your friends?" Peter asked as his men relaxed their hold.

"Lizzy fancies a spirit called Henry Adamson, not me, you know people here, give me a shaman, medium to banish Henry and his ape to hell?" Steve as a night moth landed on his forehead, its creepy crawly movement made him think how big it was, so he ate it believing no one saw him. The moth was harmless, the mosquito full of his blood was not, he now had malaria.

It flew off into the night.

Peter thought of Lizzy, when he finished with her, Steve would not get her, she would go to a brothel making money for him.

When the last fossil safely sold and Peter was rich, the sea crocodiles would have Steve, he did not need to do that, but Roger was prompting him not to leave witnesses.

Peter Jong was as bad as his ancestor.

"Come on," I said to Calamity, and both orbed to the jetty to find Lizzy on the boat, where were the two men?

I saw two spirits orbing the water, unable to accept death as it was sudden, meaning they might end up trapped here.

"You said it was only a woman," one orb shouted at the other.

"Yes, what a woman, killed us both," the other orb answered.

Crocodile eyes looked at me and Calamity wondering where our bodies where?

Lizzy when I was inside her mind, showed me when the boat was at the jetty, saw one man at the stern throwing a chicken head to a crocodile, which brought other reptiles.

"I looked for his friend, he was boiling water ready to cook the chicken, but in an instant walked to the man tormenting the crocodiles and pushed him in, one less share.

His screams cheered his attacker as it meant he would not survive to kill him. Thinking sex, he bent to enter the rattan cabin where I stabbed repeatedly with this and guided him over the side."

Lizzy brandishing a twenty-foot meat cleaver, in my mind it was that gigantic, in fact a tiny potato peeler.

That is why I am changing clothes, waiting for you two, where is Steve?" Lizzy had pictured.

"Ook," Calamity saying this was a wonder girl, glad she was on our side.

Beside Lizzy were automatic rifles and guns.

In the water her bloodied shirt, a live yellow reptilian eye watched them from under it.

"Steve has," and I told Lizzy what we had seen at Peter's dig while she buttoned clean clothes. "Judas Priest," I tried not to look, but as I was a ghost Lizzy felt safe; I mean I was not a physical man getting hot places. I sensed her wondering if I was.

"Ook," Calamity saying, "This is some woman," adding "Ook," "You dirty old Mannie."

Even in Spirit I choked for a reply as memories of a dry throat clouded me.

"I served in the army, killed enemy, get used to it, them or you, these two men or me. I am certainly not going to do nothing but scream," Lizzy told us as the river cleared of the men given to it. Later the crocodiles did give them to the mangroves as food, understand this, nothing wasted in the cycle of life.

I had pictured the scene, she was right, if she had not turned the tables, she did be dead, and the story ended.

"Ook," Calamity wrapping spirit hairy arms on Lizzy saying,

"Friend," and looking to see if Lizzy held the potato peeler.

"Ook," I imitated and wrapped oily arms about Lizzy.

"You got a couple of dimples, a cat coil of a hair strand, not to prominent Adams Apples, skinny but suppose that comes with ectoplasm stretching and what else," and looked down, "nothing there."

"Madam I assure over here amputated limbs grow back."

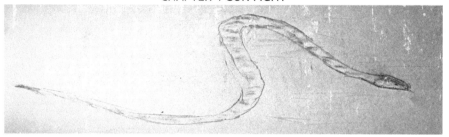

Figure 4 An original Henry Adamson drawing of a yellow banded krait, a poisonous bite, 1900, Sandakan, Borneo.

Peter had organized his men to carry the canvas bags as he followed, and behind him one rear guard whom he planned to exit this world of green creepers and lizards running up them to be away from men.

(Now the writer of the Gospel of Mary Magdalene had spoken to these lizards, 'men are supposed to be your friends, not chop you up as a curried mixed meat dish, 20% discount on this dish only today.' The author, a two-thousand-year-old ghost, awesome.

To Peter the only person going aboard his old wooden river boat was himself and if alive, Lizzy, and because Roger was possessing Peter, he arrogantly ignored myself and the ape's approach, we saw all right down to ants on the path carrying food ten times heavier than themselves.

Saw Peter drop back after a mile, silently till the rear guard caught up with him.

The man's eyes narrowed; e tried peering past Peter to see if they were alone.

"********," Something spoken in Malay and the man overtook Peter, to freeze, gasp for air and fall to his knees.

Oh, what a liar Peter you are that he told the man his friends were just behind

Peter did not have to do what he did, the man was dying, Peter had stuck his machete into his back; it had to be Roger urging him in his mind as to behead the man, once a friend, now an ex-shareholder, well that left five ahead. The ants knew men always dropped food so followed.

I really feared for Lizzy, Calamity felt the fear and agreed, "Ook." Fear was here now as Roger detecting our energies flew out of Peter as a dark mist hitting us.

"I watch American Football," Roger proud of his attack.

So sudden, Calamity bounced to the flowering treetops, and I like a snooker ball off to the left amongst wild honeycombs, smearing me in delicious ape snack.

"She is mine Henry," Roger said to me through waves of energy, zooming towards Lizzy. I followed, exactly what that ghost wanted me to do.

"Not on your nellie mate," I answered back acting tough.

2OOK,2 CALAMITY EXCITED OVER A FIGHT FOR A FEMALE, "Ook," translated, "Maybe me?"

Anyway, the white energy waves in the Ether fell silent as spirit folk became interested in us.

Peter hurried on to assume his position behind his men. It took a while as the men had reached the jetty and aghast, the old boat was gone; Lizzy had it; the boat was life, she wanted to live. Peter and his men could die for all she cared and did, cared them dead.

"Ook," Calamity MEANING, "Wonder Woman," amazed, adoring, and jealous of her looks.

Peter cursed, he had wanted to shoot them all in the back just before they got here, but then he cheered, their backs were to him. It was Roger again wanting to feed on FEAR, that the men did soon have.

Lo, because Peter was behind, he assumed the boat was here, silly man, and they were so close how could he miss?

As the nearest fell, others turned to fight, retreating into the river, forgetting what waited for them. Soon the jungle filled with screams and the water thrashed with crocodiles.

On the branches above a ghost ape was using scooped out melons to try as brassieres. For panties, a leaf front and back, "Ook," which means, "Wonder Ape now."

Now Lizzy had stopped creeping towards Peter, it was dark, snakes were slithering past her feet every forty feet, and it was just too dense to advance. Safety was back at the boat. Why was she sneaking through mud to reach Peter, 'The better to eat him up,' I replied as the Big bad Wolf from red Riding Hood. Well, she was bringing the war to Peter who did not expect such a move, yes, a 'Wonder Woman'.

"Ook," "And Wonder Ape."

And Roger waited as a black mist in the wheelhouse, what wheelhouse, the wheel was under a giant umbrella with Micky Mouse plastered on it. Other Disney characters were stuck on the boats side, someone liked Disney, my there was Pluto, Donald.

And Lizzy gingerly trod back to the boat, waiting for a lethal snake bite. The mud was heaving with life, insects, leeches now on her, mosquitoes on her limbs, leeches creeping onto her bum, leeches, a thousand on her, so wisely retreated to the boat.

"Ook," Calamity appearing to any snake and spider that after seeing her, well, fled, 'What a good ape.'

"I will light the path Lizzy," and used my orb energy to do just that. Not brazenly lamp bright, but enough for Lizzy to see where her feet went, to that spot ahead where a slithering tail was. "What possessed you to enter the jungle?" I asked in her mind. A mind under control and not panicking.

"To take Peter out and be safe, and those fossils are yours," she replied seeing the sandbar and the biggest crocodile ever lounging next to the boat, it wanted fed.

Shots rang out, Peter, he was thinking of swimming to the sandbank and the boat. Why he sprayed the nearby waters with bullets, especially if yellow eyes watched him.

"Ook," Calamity watching the spirit reptiles drift away before sucked into a vortex of light to take them to their realm. I watched the leeches on Lizzy.

Satisfied, Peter out of habit rolled up his trousers to keep them dry, and Wels catfish attracted to male human legs might swallow him for us?

No such luck, from one of the dead bodies he took folded rubber, a small flier's raft from WW11, and from another a rucksack, a small gas cylinder, Peter thought of everything. He had a spiritual adviser, just like mediums, Chief Yellow Hawk, he had his ancestor Roger the Stinker DeJong.

And Lizzy had her leeches that she spent half an hour de leeching herself.

*

Peter's grandmother had been a local, a tea house owner, pretty with cash to attract Roger DeJong. Against advice she wanted Roger to what she thought was the next social level, how mistaken she was, Roger had no friends in the ruling elite, his friends were thieves, murderers.

As a journalist in last century Sandakan, stories were of pirate atrocities, the bread and butter of newspapers, but not enough pay to keep Roger in the Seafront Hotel, mingling with those that counted, the men in tight European clothes that made you sweat, and women in dresses with huge artificial bottoms and parasols and straw hats trailing long colored ribbons, that stray chow dogs grabbed, pulling, meaning they used the artificial bottoms as launching pads.

This led to the formation of the local Dog Pound and Dog Catchers.

The men had straw hats too, minus ribbons, safe from chows but not monkeys that dropped from tree branches to steal and wear in imitation.

Poor Roger, the more he mingled and played snooker with red balls, the more he bought the rounds as a lousy shot, the more he slept with wives, the more he wanted back to Europe. The fool, he had all here, a loyal pretty wife whose heart he continually broke, stories to rival Peter Pan and Moby Dick as a columnist in a local paper, but he was obsessed with Europe.

So, that he filled his children with European fables, a watercolor wash of exaggerated rot. Rot that eventually filled Peter with ambition.

But he did leave his descendants a robber network and a smart woman that took over when Roger lost his head, to the Dayaks. His wife knew her tables and that meant a calculating brain. Was she glad he met a terrifying end, yes, all that sleeping about he had contracted syphilis?

Roger's shrunk head rested on a sharp pole outside a long house, looking at the Japanese Patrol from Sandakan, who knew if that could happen to a European, it could happen to them, and did on a large scale, the Dayaks sided with the British.

 Roger was not lonely anymore, Japanese solder heads cluttered about his, all staring out at the green background of painted mountains, counting passing fruit bats.

See Peter grew up with, stories of antiheroes, of men who stole, murdered, and pimped. Nothing about good folk, so looked up to madams, and not angelic father figures. Whereas other children had Goldilocks, Shrek, Peter Rabbit and Super Man, poor Peter had peasant folklore about were-wolves, Frankenstein the Monster, and Russian Big Foot tales, and a fear of darkened spaces, so much he pushed himself to become a young Godfather. Instead of horse heads he put crocodile heads in people's beds to lubricate them into paying protection cash.

Unfortunately, a handful of crocodiles were still alive, that was bad for business.

Why Peter saw Lizzy as a commodity, a tin of coconut oil to sell, Peter had no depth of character apart from his Marianna Trench of badness.

*

"You can have the fossils, no good to me dead?" I joked with Lizzy as she stood looking at the boat, rippling river colliding gently with the rudder.

Little green fishes gathered here for shelter.

A poisonous brown water snake swam by.

Further out thick scaly monsters who swam this river when dinosaurs walked places. In deeper river parts, whiskered catfish felt for food.

"Why thank you Henry," it was the way she thanked, it stirred me, making me think she liked me. Where was the hair gel to smarten up?

"Ook," Calamity making fun of me. My apish friend was right, could I stir, I lacked important thingamabobs, I was a **GHOST.**

"You were a handsome man when alive Henry, Roger stole your dream, I will get the fossils back in your name, the fame yours, the remembrance also," Lizzy with a steamy cat look promising. "Woof," she had forgotten LINGERIE thankfully.

I ask you, who was this woman? She took care of two guards on the boat. Nothing she thought was impossible, especially when the boat meant life. She is toying with the idea of a ghostly relationship. She thought nothing impossible, always a first; and admit I was blown away, had she forgotten I was a ghost? Afraid, yes, too right, Lizzy was a physical, *'me Tarzan ghost she jane, ha.'*

"Henry, what is there to be afraid?" She thought back.

"Ook," an apish remark, "Because he is my husband," the

lying monkey.

"I entered her consciousness opening a portal, so she saw the magnificence of Spirit, the vibrance, life, Spirit was not dead, either was I. She saw Calamity blowing raspberries at her, and when noticed at me, to Calamity this was Wonder Woman, could get away with anything except me.

"Ook," Calamity alerting us to a dark mist on the boat, forming into the face of Roger. Between us ghosts, he was more handsome, but he smelt bad, darkness always does.

"What a stink?" Lizzy offending Roger who could not smell himself as he imagined himself covered in bath salts, the way he used to be. They had head lice back then and looked, that infuriated Roger, made him forget Calamity.

"Ook," Calamity seeing the human who had shot her and attacked.

"I had better help," I said to Lizzy who did not stand idly by, but as myself **and Calamity locked consciousness with Roger,** she went to start the boat engine, mobility would give a sense of control.

Why none of us heard the paddling of Peter as he drew alongside, the paddle scattering the little fish out into the open river as food for Perch, they in turn eaten by crocodiles; and he made his first mistake, he threw the canvas bags containing Ramapithecus, my fossils onto the boat to me.

"Help Peter help," it was Steve shouting from the jetty that alerted us to Peter's presence.

"Stupid man," Peter hissed since discovered; what had he to worry about, it was only Lizzy, a woman he faced. Black leaches clung to his uncovered legs; his soles had no friction so slipped on the smooth boats deck.

A long "WA," as he went up and shorter "WA" as he landed heavily on his bottom.

"And us," I shouted in his head meaning Calamity too, "Ook," she added from across the river where Roger had fought her and zoomed back. Peter covered his ears and collapsed to his knees shinning them; germs, this was the tropics.

"Henry," it was Roger coming to his descendant's aid. How could such a handsome face belie the evil lurking underneath. Why it melted into attacking darkness, the energy hitting me like a water buffalo knocking me into the jungle, stopping beside a python waiting for dinner, an antelope wanting a drink, which startled cleared off and the python try as might could not coil me as I was just mist, "hiss," the departing angry snake, "Where is Steve?"

Lizzy felt the mental pain as our link broke.

Peter got up, slipping still, so held the boat's low railing, making him bend, forcing his eyes to focus on the water snake swimming about after little disturbed fish.

That water would claim Lizzy when he finished with her and smiled, not a thought for Steve.

Silly Peter, Lizzy grew up on stories of the Old West, to be independent. She also had gone to the college self-defense classes; no match for Peter's Kung Fu, but it illustrates her life attitude, and to use the heavy stolen red fire extinguisher Peter kept aboard his wooden boat.

I need not have worried about her, yes ghosts do try and protect the living from bad entities, you see, we can worry in the After Life. No twisted thoughts of, "If Peter kills her, she will be with me in Spirit. I will join with her as energy," which is the way we well share melons in The After Life.

As it was, I do little as Roger kept hitting me with energy he was directing to Lizzy, I was a shield. Now she was worried for me, for it is a true saying, "Think of someone, and you will attract that person." So was aware Lizzy was thinking of me, so was Roger who made intimidating slurs about Lizzy to me.

Worried as she had seen the size of the dark orb come from Peter and drag me away. She had no intention of joining me in the After Life, her world was full of colored butterflies, squirrels stealing your peanuts left on the park bench. Of racoons knocking over bins and feasting on thrown out triple cheese pizzas. These days, Sandakan has pizza parlors, a bustling modern city.

Having a romantic fling with a ghost as a new thingamabob to try was one thing but coming to live with that ghost another. Lizzy was all fighting pioneer woman; Peter beware that Midwest tornado was coming to you.

"Ook," Calamity now reassuring Lizzy she was not alone as the ape surrounded her with her own Spirit Light, "Ook."

"What are those?" Lizzy pointing at Calamity's melon brasserie.

Anyway, it came as a black blur, and was heavy, see Peter liked frying his chop suey and, "Ook," Calamity winching as his wok thud into his head as Lizzy delivered it. Not a trace of cooking fell from the wok, Peter was obsessed with cleanliness, see the fire hydrant was too heavy to swing as a baseball bat.

Not even an "Ouch," or, "Oh that hurt," escaped Peter's lips, well, he sorts of stood there wobbling.

Lizzy came right up to him and blew into his face, then spat just before she with fingers helped him backwards so, gravity took over; away he went into the darkness, lit by yellow and red eyes of hungry predators watching us. She did not want him aboard wakening to be a threat again, he was better with them, those things swimming about, crocodiles and snakes.

"Ook," meaning, "my heroine."

Oh bother, what a lucky man Peter was bouncing onto his inflatable and not acrobatically going into the running river, well, where the boat was, tepid, so quick came mosquitoes, and since he was in Nether Land, *had to accept them taking twenty pints of his blood!*

Big dark, even small ones, crocodiles began exercising amongst themselves as they bit others in frustration their diner was not in their tummies.

"Peter," Roger wailed believing him dead, killed by this woman, and he used up energy so even the leopard on the tree heard him.

A jolly good thing too, as enabled Lizzy to stand Roger off and Calamity bounce white light into him.

"Ook," Calamity having the time of her apish life.

Then silence dropped like the final theatre curtain on the river.

"Ook," Calamity amazed Roger dimmed, so allowed her attention drawn to Lizzy and Peter, ah the bad man slept like a baby, a baby with a fractured jaw, cheeks, and vacant teeth slots, *indeed woks are heavy!*

As a side kick Calamity stayed close to Lizzy, Roger was eternally alive, defeated only.

"Splash," as Lizzy cast aside the mooring rope she hacked, the end tied about a small anchor on the sand could stay there, why already little sand crabs were making homes in the dented sand, and slithering in the water, that brown water snake thinking the watered rope a friend and romance.

The boat began to sway a little as the river current took the hull, as for Peter, his inflatable was spinning away to the jetty followed by yellow eyes.

On the jetty Steve looked about for a place to hide, he did not think of surrendering, then asking mercy, just to hide in the darkness which is his new comfortable friend.

Then he saw the dropped weapons amongst the land crabs. Where should I go, rifles or crabs, I do like crabs, and need the rifles for protection," he puzzled.

As for Peter, Steve does what he was thinking of doing as a

crocodile had taken the inflatable's rope and began to drag the craft onto the sand, where it would devour the sleeping, Peter.

Steve wanted to run, also part of him wanted to stay and watch Peter eaten and be sure he was dead, then he remembered the weapon he held, it gave him power, he was master, so stood up too quickly and the crab rough bits went down dry, and he coughed repeatedly, alerting the crocodile to his presence, it hissed at him, and something bigger hissed back from the jungle edge.

Steve shot the reptile dead; Calamity nervously watched the reptile spirit rise out of the dead crocodile, apes and these creatures were not friends, then the new spirit crossed into Spirit Realms.

Then Calamity went berserk on Steve, rubbing him of his new mental confidence as she hit him with tennis sized energy balls. The old Steve reappeared, and he ran into the jungle, 'to be or not to be eaten?'

"Ook," Calamity not wasting energy to run down the retreating and so went to look for me.

"Henry," Lizzy calling for me. Awakening me, Light was greater than Darkness, and just as well as she was wakening Roger out of his defeated state of consciousness. Like cannonball ferocity I blew into his orb that was gathering dark strength to possess Lizzy *and make her go for a swim.*

Roger found the Light entered closets he did not want opened and secrets out, whatever dark powers had come to his aid fled, Light is Greater than Darkness *and sold under names, Dash, Sparkle Clean, Eco wash, ah a ghost can joke and get away with it.*

"Ook," Calamity assuring Lizzy there was a smart ghost and a human, how could they lose?

"Henry, I feel many bad spirits coming to aid Roger, what are we to do?" Lizzy asked.

"Start the engine and flee," I said in her mind, "and throw figs their way, sure Calamity can manage them," I was being flippant as love of that woman lifted me to heights of endurance, I was about to *die* taking on those dark powers alone.

Wait a mo., I am dead, they cannot hurt me, *let us get them Calamity, I knew I was dead all along.*

"Ook," Calamity joining me putting up a barrier of Light to protect the boat and Lizzy, *the remark about figs would be cast up in a quitter unsuspecting relaxing moment; "Ook, where are my figs?"*

"Hummer hum," went the engine coughing out breathing problems.

Lizzy looked nice screwing her eyes up against black oily smoke. I had better be careful as she became aware I was staring.

"Ook," Calamity poking me to concentrate on her conversation, "Ook," "figs," she was saying.

ANYWAY: Ghosts can know fear, I did not die a fearful man, I had never shown fear in the local militia comprised of locals, Dutch and British too, Eurasians, when the whistle blew to charge the pirates lounging on the beach with shanghaied girls, confiscated custom liquor, cooked meats sold by street vendors and more we charged.

We attackers wanted an end to this thievery, why, an honest shoe boy wanted his trade essentials back as he was going hungry.

Fear, you put aside, tensed, stopped thinking, you had a job to do, and when the fighting was over, even then fear did not come; it was a job, just like Lizzy killing those two men on the boat, a job to survive.

"Ook," Calamity knowing fear of humankind, humans that shot orangutan mothers to steal the babies. Of humans who burnt down forests to grow palm trees.

But these dark entities were spirits, human bad men friends of Roger who she hated, and hate overcame Calamity's fear.

As the boat pulled away from this dark curtain that could not penetrate myself and Calamity's Light barrier, *rescuing angels appeared?*

"Is that a trumpet?" Lizzy at the wheel puzzled.

She heard the call, not angelic, but my old friends from the militia, and those dark orbs the enemy needing a spiritual bashing.

"Ook," an excited Calamity watching about a hundred white glowing orbs come out of riverside portals, gateways humans never knew existed. Militiamen dressed in period uniforms, a bit tattered and spooky, but friends.

"I hate you Henry, hate you," Roger as he fled to the 7th Level of Hell? Where the gnashing of teeth happens, also that horrid wailing. He did not get that far; he certainly did not flee to the Light, so where did he go?

*

The sky was clear, now we saw white stars, downriver a good distance, Lizzy did not want to steer the boat in the darkness, even with a stolen strobe light, daylight was safer.

Why them yellow eyes reminded you if you fell in you was a goner, for a living person, not me and Calamity, we were dead already.

"Forgive me Father Spirit for I killed men, if I had time, I did have maimed instead, thank you for my company, protect Henry and Calamity, bring them home always, love Lizzy, Amen," she spoke aloud, why not, the fireflies liked what she said, they buzzed faster knocking mosquitoes out.

"I really liked that bit about 'home,' thank you Lizzy," and thanked the eternal throbbing energy that made us spirit folk prime in years again.

Yep, I spruced up, out came hair gel, hairbrush, after shave, oxer orange essence pong to make me more handsome, than Roger and Peter.

"Pt," Calamity replying, and I gummed my lips as if I lacked teeth, well, I did lack an entire physical body did I not?

"I like you Henry, and Roger seems powerful, do you mind turning your back?" She asked, Judas Priest I had forgotten human needs, and obeyed and' "Roger mentioned again."

"Ook," Calamity misting up so I could see nothing if I wanted, girls stuck together. Oh well I settled down near the generator whose rubber belt span quickly, feeding me and Calamity depleted energy.

"Whack, whack, whack," went the rubber belt. Flying bugs sucked into the belts spin zoomed away at a million miles an hour to the other side of the river, right into the thousands of enormous bird eating spider webs. Bug or bird, both tasty to a competitive spider with lot hungry relations near you.

I was in thought, Lizzy's strawberry perfume put me back to another world, where I had hoped to purchase a house with strawberries in the backyard.

Lizzy liked me, so what, people liked people, but I was a ghost, I could not use her to replace the wife I never had a hundred years ago.

"Why not?" It was Lizzy, I had forgotten she was mediumistic and had linked into my mind. I sweated, Lizzy knew I liked her lots, I was embarrassingly happy as if caught stealing strawberries and managed to eat half.

"Ook," Calamity feeling my thoughts, she had two children, and saddened us, for humans had taken them to sell in the exotic animal market. Her husband, the healthiest at the time and what was his name again? "Ook, Smelly Bum," or was it, "Ook, Smelly Feet," Calamity did not want to remember, hunters shot him to get the young.

She would like to see him in Spirit once our trouble settled down, get his name right, "Ook," and huggees apes liked, then call out for the young, if they were dead, they did answer. Poor Calamity, which was over a hundred years ago.

"How sad Calamity?" Lizzy pushing back the frail rainbow pigment beaded curtain to the makeshift cabin.

Even though the paraffin lamp behind her gave Lizzy a glowing aurora filled with flying bugs, making her angelic, I was panicking, if she had understood Calamity's sadness, she would have read me, 'could she like me a little extra?' If she had, said nothing, I sighed energetic relief, so hundreds of tiny white orbs left me, competing with the bugs in her aurora.

"What are we sighing about Henry?" Lizzy asked as if she did not know?

So, shriveled, as a heel should, like one of those dead men who had sexual desires towards her.

Then she appeared in my conscious mind smiling, then gone.

The ancient game was on, if any had sexual intentions it was Lizzy, like stated, she was game for anything.

Guess who appeared next, "Ook," you were right.

Then splashing as a log drifted by, should have investigated but to wrapped up in High School ways. Remember the log, was it a log or something more devilish?

"Think we are safe here for the night Henry?" She ordered and asked simultaneously, ah this 'Henry' stuff was 'Lullabying' me as if opium smoke had drifted upriver to us from Sandakan dens.

"We have codeine tablets these days Henry," Lizzy, see entrancing me, and the log was gone followed by diners.

What protectors me and Calamity were?

"Ook," Calamity agreeing, 'Oh that ape certainly popped up

uninvited, "Ook."

So not arguing we silently watched Lizzy open a tin of Irish Stew, although she was vegetarian in habits, emergency demanded energy. Calamity ate strawberries given by me, and I ate vegetarians to impress Lizzy. The important thingmabob was, we ate together in consciousness, which was leading to other thoughts about girls and ghosts sort of stuff. I now clear my throat.

"Think it was duck Henry? What a pig, ate it all up, not a morsel left for you," and was jolly, and after prompting, 'Ook,' Calamity joined in, oh what a happy band of adventurers we were?

"Better not," I advised misting over her left hand playing in the river to wash the plate and pulled her arm up quick.

Yellow eyes appeared, peeved where the owners of the mouths below cheated dinner.

"Now a powerful question answered," as she was playing with the plate, "I felt your energy Henry, it lifted my hand," and she thought Henry as a spook might be a great lover, "mummy," I mumbled.

I was no Steve in her mind, more aligned to her independent ways of thinking, "Ook," again.

"We will find out some night?" Lizzy, what else could I reply, "HUMBUGS?"

"Ook," Calamity excited hoping for babies to check for fleas in their fur and them hers.

"Human babies are furless," I started to explain, sighed, and fell silent, "MINT HUMBUGS," and knew did have to produce them for Calamity to try.

"Lizzy had a good, excited laugh, Calamity of course added, 'Ook.'

Anyway: to skip the romantic bit, you know where girl flicks a firefly at boy, who grunts and jumps excitedly so, the boat cap- sizes keeping the crocodiles happy.

Lizzy went to bed on the worn-out Peter mattress, we all headed to a bed, even ghosts need a rest, R.I.P., a joke, spirits can do that as well.

The only good thing Peter left here was the mosquito net, ignored at your peril for malaria and nasty bugs awaited you in an inflamed itchy swollen red bite.

"Ook," Calamity took over the watch, the crocodiles stared back, disliking her, Calamity was a ghost, reminding them they could become leather shoes.

"Henry," Lizzy called as the jungle filled with sounds, like that hungry leopard; yeh she knew I heard her, I was a ghost, those yawning leopards and flying fruit bats might give a phys- ical a deaf excuse, but I had none against her mediumistic tal- ents., "mummy," I squeaked as like Steve had spent my whole life in jungles, in other words, I was well, well, a, a MINT HUMBUG.

Woof, what talents to, "What are you waiting for Henry?" I asked myself and drifted through the mosquito netting. No sense knocking and what an attractive woman in those green standard Harrison Ford jungle clothes.

Well, I just orbed, had no physical form, what IF I had a body? Would I have remained motionless, staring at the lady, making all feel uncomfortable?

"Henry, I can see you, think you could have shaved and showered first?" Lizzy in the semi darkness of the paraffin lamp.

"Ook," Calamity agreeing.

That made me hesitate, what do ghosts smell of? "Sniff, sniff," electricity, of an electric train engine, "Sniff," so imagined the flowers of a meadow.

I smelled good now.

Lizzy laughed, so did an ape, so did I, oh our happy threesome, THREESOME?

"Ook," Calamity no longer watching the river, so I thought wild figs, honeycombs, bananas, melons and more and dumped it on her orb, then closed my mind to her as this was a twosome so, Calamity away with you.,

AND TO YOU but will tell you a little.

I dropped my orb onto her body, all right spirit possession, my hundred-year-old vampire fangs flopped out., bet you believe me?

Lizzy opened her consciousness to mine, our minds join. She sees me, thankfully that continually vibrating power on my side, spirits call God, made me look healthy, human, not a moldy corpse.

I call this energy one of the Faces of God, an attribute of God, whatever would not a human President like to own it? So, beautiful Lizzy saw me as a full-bodied man, not a see-through spook with vampire teeth and empty black eye sockets. Told you, floppy vampire fangs.

So, our conscious minds became one, union, and the mind is a powerful tool. In Spirit if I want a chocolate cake, I get one, with the tastiest cocoa ever.

Look, Sherlock Holmes's creator son, killed in the trenches of the Great European War, sent a message he was smoking and drinking, it is MIND that survives; Spirit must be a type of Greater Mind Consciousness, and not up to me to try and figure anything more out, I have a story to tell.

Just that I was a real man in Lizzy's mind, and she knew she had entered a new world of finely tuned emotion. In Spirit all has a newness, of smell, color, touch, sounds, and imagination that I urge you to use.

And my nerves went out with the rubber vampire fangs, a woman was nothing to be afraid of except the ape variety.

"Ook," Calamity stopping the thought train, she was pointing at canvas bags, my bags were home.

"Ook," again and pointed at the river, it was clear of crocodiles, what did it mean? Where had they gone, to an easier meal?

So, Calamity and I rested near the boat's electric generator, absorbing energy, we also had the rippling river and water has always been a source of Spirit.

Lucozade to us two.

As for the canvas bags, forgotten as all needed rest, mm, even the fruit bats as the orange sun were coming out.

*

Now Peter had to thank Steve, who had rescued him putting him in the inflatable and so it was Steve's splashing that we heard as he passed the boat. The splashing had brought the crocodilian diners after him, so we had none to watch us breakfast.

Also, he was too far away for us to hear him, "Naughty reptiles, stop eating my paddles, bad crocodiles, Steve getting angry, Steve mighty hungry."

And these two lost men saved by tribal folk going to Sandakan in their outboard canoes, full of jungle produce, shrunken heads, caged songbirds, baby monkeys, snakes for gall bladder drinking, also healthy jungle fruits, figs, honey, orchids.

In return did go home with pots, pans, and fuel for cooking and two heads for shrinking.

Yes sir, Steve was a lucky man that day, "Peter," one of those locals, knowing the villain, also the reward they did get from Peter when he awoke, and he did pay, or they did sneak up to him as Bogeymen.

They did not take him to the local hospital as that would involve questions and police, so sent one of their own into the jetties where you could by a Sumatran Rhino for cash. To find the brothers,

cousins of those who had gone with Peter, to look after Peter, but the Dayaks said naught that Peter had killed his friends but did say," Not leaving till get cash."

The Dayaks wanted sacks of pans, forks, water bottles, holed beads for necklaces, biros, Brill pads, bullets, bras and such frillies the girls would like and hard cash.

As for Steve he spoke about ghosts, snakes, Lizzy, and an ape that "Ook," so thought he was insane and allowed him to come along. The more Steve spoke, the Dayaks' learned Peter was unnecessary luggage.

Well done, Steve, kill Peter off.

The Dayaks thought Steve a good fly and bug killer, so started making a collar and lead for him, and started to argue which long house Steve to belong to at night, as a mosquito trap, for he ate them.

These people did realize Steve was a lost dark soul and would bring Dayak horror legends out of the jungle to them so wanted rid of this maniac.

Borneo's were-creatures, shape shifters.

Boogiemen with sticky vine hands at the end of creeps.

Rabid bats by the dozen as cheaper that way.

The souls of Japanese soldiers seeking the rest of their bodies.

"Thank you, Steve," these people did say remembering the idiot that ate flies.

Book 2

The Haunted Plane.

*Figure 5 Taken by a street photographer, **Lizzy**, Sandakan, 2021. The youth could not afford color films.*

Lizzy sat in a window seat first class looking at the speeding clouds, well she could afford first, see, Lizzy had inherited a Ranch in Montana, so was loaded, which meant nothing to me as dead, "Ook," Calamity wanting to ride horses, and secondly myself and Calamity had come along, we did not need to, we could have thought ourselves to New York along the thought spider web circling Earth; that is how I describe it, an internet of thought.

Each spirit touching its neighbor as a spider's web, thus a thought travelling along at fantastic speed. "Hey Calamity, let us visit Bondi Beach as bored," I think to my friend and we think, or I do as Calamity has no idea what that beach is, so she hops into my thought and I think Australia," and no sooner thought than I am there.

I enter a beach boy's head and look through his eyes at the wonders of life cluttering the sand, burning their skin off under a hot sun. Calamity follows and the youth "Ook," runs like, a well APE, as Calamity is inside his head. Then a big "OOK," as Calamity sees a kangaroo and falls in love.

Or can do it hard way reaching Australia, jump into a portal, and come out the other end, sure to be a portal at Bondi?

"Ook," Calamity wrestling with a kangaroo trying to push the beast into our portal, and the kangaroo leaps away as is a physical.

"Ook," Calamity heart broken.

Anyway, interlude over, the thought web, millions of spirit minds connected, speed is the essence of Spirit; Is Spirit a Mind? Is the constant vibration in Light, this, Mind? Spirits describe that vibration making you young, is so fast not slow, that is the medicine of eternal youth, I guess? Lucky for humankind eternal youth found in a Near Death Experience, unlucky for you rejected by whoever? A walk to the corner shop in physical might take twenty minutes, in Spirit a nano second and less.

All I know Calamity and self can think and summon memories out of this Spirit that vibrates so fast, so ask the question, do we live in the MIND of something?

Eternal SIM toys that we are?

Needless Calamity's memories are bananas, figs, wild honeycombs, and male apes. Mine, archaeology newsletters, chef cook aids, venomous snake guides, post cards.

So, now I have explained why we were on a plane, no I have not, well, I wanted next to Lizzy even if I hated flying; also, we were lazy, better to lounge in first class than the hassle of going through portals and realms to be there before Lizzy. The food we could taste because as Lizzy ate, we obtained the essences, flavors, the pongs of coffee and cream, nice.

Also, I was a man of the paddle wheel masted ships, flying was for birds and spirits, ha, like Calamity, and all right me, I could fly those thought waves, but Lizzy would be absent; think I had developed strong feelings for her.

If you can love, you are close to whatever God is, The Energy of Love, Electromagnetism, so hug a neighbor and get beat up, ha, another Spirit joke, bad taste, yes?

We take our memories and feelings over when we die, over where? To the After- Life, where memories can be dark, and Light, so watch that film 'Ghost,' with Patrick Swayze that is truthful to the point we live with folks like Calamity and self, and shows him going into the Light, and the bad evil villain taken by dark hoodies, the crocodiles of Sandakan.

Well, when that dark villain dies, he cannot just walk into the Light. He is a shade of grey.

Hear told hospitals exist in The After Life for sick spirits that need cleaning, who knows, I never went to one.

"Ook," Calamity agreeing summoning figs topped with pine-apple ice cream; a result of tasting human food in Lizzy's mind.

Anyway: as it was dark and a long-haul flight, we took Lizzy on our own long flight, as a guest, she was still alive, she left her body, her breathing almost stopped, that quiet. The first thing she noticed was how dark it was, yes, we were in the Ether, the immediate padding about us, and took a while for her to notice spirit folk sittings about the plane.

We were not the only spirits out of our bodies in this flight, why they were on the earth realm was their business.

Anyway, Lizzy into a realm that was not all Light, like the settling dusk, here birds and Rock Pigeons cleaned their feathers as wash before bed. She could not enter true The Light as she was not dead, is what I believe, her body's chest still rose and fell with a heartbeat.

"Ook," translated, "perve."

Lots birds sang here, and the pigeons gobbled between them-selves, 'My eggs are whiter than yours,' 'rubbish my chick is more yellow,' 'my chicks will be voted prettiest in the realm,' long before human physicals except no opposing thumb and speak gibberish?

A wolverine climbed down branches ignoring the pigeon pie.

It saw us and focused on Lizzy, knowing she was not truly dead, then if a wolverine smiled, it did and went wherever?

Then music heard, as IF Sea Cows were singing backed up by whale songs. It took hold of you, flushed out toxins, then left you a brighter light. Music restored 'junk' that you had thrown away as is energy and not destroyed, just stored away in a different form.

A painting by you in the attic, a rejected manuscript you burned, it is all here in AWESOMENESS; is what we call God, a memory BANK? "Ook," meaning **what we say,** every thought, every deed is recorded in The Hall of Records in Heaven, "Ook," Calamity dismissing thoughts of stealing physical bananas from the airplane galley.

"Ook," adding "I am a good girl."

Roger and Peter be careful you are not those villains in that Patrick Swayze film 'Ghost?'

As we left Lizzy kept looking back like Lot's wife, except she did not turn to stone, but marveled at the wisdom collected in this realm since time started, or since a spark of LIFE moved across slime somewhere in the universe collecting memories, died and its consciousness took residence in The Light, the first high being, all other slime movers were below its consciousness.

Just thoughts as The After Life is a deliberate puzzle.

"Ook."

Lizzy stopped, she was watching rats like lemmings streaming towards The Light, happy and eager to get there. At first Lizzy retreated inwards, brought up those rats were dirty disease spreading critters, "Such yucky creatures here in heaven?" Lizzy thought.

"All are made of the same spirit, so all come back to that spirit," it vibrated through her and us, it was God, That Spirit teaching her over here they are clean intelligent loving animals.

Lizzy looked again but she had no eyes, they were back in her body, and saw all the rats were orbs of beautiful light not fresh out of sewers with loo paper clinging to them.

Smiling all refreshed we took Lizzy to that library that holds records of all things, here curiosity took hold of her as she wanted to know if a thesis, she wrote about diseases spreading from monkeys to humans, yes here, as rejected on Earth.

Yes, it was, and full of giggles she held up her sketching pads of childish drawings, nothing is wasted, it was needed for 'LIFE REPLAYS.'

"Sort of evidence room when we are called to the, well I call them Elders, where our life is recycled Infront of us. I have no record here," afraid my badness did drive her away, forgetting my goodness did bring her back, I was being a child.

"No, you don't," Lizzy alarmed I was hiding traits I was an obsessive eater of cream cakes, a lingerie collector, she had not forgotten, like Calamity wanting her 'figs.'

"Ook," Calamity as her jealous mind wanted to know, and cast more rotten figs my way for not thinking of her in same light.

The answer was simple, "Calamity dear, you are an ape and I a human spirit," and did not include 'ugly monkey dear.'

To prove a point, we took Lizzy to a flowering bush where we could look between the purple, white and orange rhododendron flowers. There a male spirit taken out of his cozy family group resting on a bluish cloud to an auditorium filled with, his relatives, friends, those he hurt, and ELDERS, angelic spirits of a higher mentality.

Funeral march music played loudly for effect, well, MIND was in a jolly mood.

Anyway, the fool thought he was to watch a movie, he was, his life and soon he was squirming as looking in disbelief at the horrid cruel acts he did in the physical. He had not been kind but taking, and at the end screaming in terror sent back to the physical to the thumbs down of the audience and to the misery of the living.

Was he coming back as a victim of his boot from his previous life, the dog he starved? Now "Ook," we could see Lizzy was worried, thinking that our ghostly relationship a sin?

"Not all are reincarnated Lizzy, he has been shown mercy," I whispered to Lizzy, "getting another chance."

"Ook," Calamity agreeing, "Ook," showing other places he could have gone in Spirit?

I remembered a scene where a murdered child is led by angels to the physical to live her life, again a merciful act of God.

As for the murderer, unrepentant monkey, whoops, I mean scorpion, he progressed down levels of darkness, to the seventh, where it is DARK, no light, just moaning and gnashing of false and real teeth.

Oh well, the murderer would be happy here as he would meet the same minds as his own, an act of love by God.

Now Calamity and I took a hand of Lizzy each and sped to a heaven of colors not seen on Earth, and the music that touched a soul.

"Ook," Calamity even enjoying this high-pitched whale song.

"Hospitals, for those needing touching up before going into The Light, look Lizzy," and we looked and saw billions standing, sitting, floating listening to the unseen whale.

Angels walked amongst them healing.

We stayed a long time, but time here is fast so forgot planes land and now hovering fly like outside Lizzy's body, wondered why passengers were alarmed over Lizzy's deadly grey appearance; and just as well the plane had not landed or they did have slid Lizzy down an emergency shoot to an ambulance; as long as Lizzy was off the plane so the cleaners could start seeking fallen cash; they had kid birthdays, funerals, divorces, expensive solicitor bills, monthly electric scooter payments, high electric bills, so, forgive and be blessed.

Now being curious paused next to a shaft of wonderous LIGHT instead of pushing Lizzy back to the physical.

"Ook," Calamity wanting Lizzy pushed back to the physical as a suspicious jealous ape mind was surfacing, I was going to make Lizzy stay our side, but I only wanted her to see as much of **my** world as possible.

"Ook," oh dear "meant **OUR** world," and peeled the rotten fruit off my orb just thrown.

"How many times do I remind you, me you friend, you me not never mind, me no ape, but ape human," confusing both as knowing I was thinking rubbish as both knew strange relationships form in Spirit? Why that hamster went off with that rat as loved each other, love being the KEY? Why fig syrup was pored over me by a monkey, quick, I mean ape.

"I am being drawn to the top," Lizzy said, "can we go there?"

"No, that is the 14th level of heaven, we are at level 3, where Saint Paul learned the secrets of heaven and talked to angels, look Lizzy," and she looked straight ahead, and if a lift door opened, we saw into level 3. It was blue and whitish light, billions more souls here, dead physicals came here; and frightenedly watched a steady stream of ELDERS taking souls for a life review. Reminding Lizzy of a queue of cattle electrically prodded into a slaughterhouse, and as we three musketeers linked saw the fear in the human cattle.

Angels came to us, who said they were sexless, did they

not once mate with Earth woman and have giants as offspring? There was hope for me and Lizzy and more rotten figs thrown.

From angel eyes we saw they came from a realm of Light Energy where they were born to serve God, The vibrating Light? They had wings as we expected them to have wings, breathily we saw their worlds, radiant gold energy bands and planets with giant fountains of musical Light, and flowers mm, the scent, so large became beds of rest.

Then we were back on the plane, whatever Saint Paul learned about level three, edited in the early years of Christianity. We had not learned any secrets that a soul coming back from a Near Death Experience would not tell.

Coming back to Lizzy's body we passed spirits trapped outside The Light, lost fighter pilots still fighting, needing rescued, told them their wars had ended, could go home, HOME, The Wonderous Light.

Then Lizzy woke, refreshed and energetic, mischief more like as did not want to sit anymore, but jump for joy The Dance of King David, fortunately clothed.

"What drugs have you taken?" A woman flight attendant realistically.

Remarkably Lizzy now saw the spirit folk sitting next to live physicals on the plane, most relations of the travelers protecting them. The others, well, attachments, greasy spirits likening that girl too much, wanting that man drunk, filling another's mind with thoughts of Red-Light areas he could visit.

Greasy was not the word, as Saint Paul said, 'they are just waiting to drag us down.'

A devil on one shoulder and an angel on the other, well, greasy spirit attachments.

"What's this?" Lizzy asking about a silver cord that came out of her body and entered the Ether.

"If it snaps you are dead like us," I replied urging her away in case accidents occur, "It's in the bible also, "when the golden vessel breaks," your body, you will be with us. As it says, *"Or ever the **silver cord** be loosed. Then shall the dust return to the earth as it was: and the spirit shall return unto God who gave it (Ecclesiastes 12:6-7)."*

"Ecclesiastes 12:6 Remember Him before the silver cord is broken and the golden bowl is crushed, the pitcher by the well is shattered and the wheel at the cistern is crushed.

As Saint Paul said Lizzy, "I know a man in Christ who fourteen years ago was caught up to the third heaven, whether in the body or out of the body I do not know, God knows, and he heard things that cannot be told, which man may not utter, 'On behalf of this man I will boast, but on my behalf I will not boast.

How he was "caught up into paradise and heard unspeakable things, which it is not lawful for a man to utter," Lizzy and "he spoke to angels in the third level of heaven."

It looks rather fragile; does it play heavy music?" Lizzy being whimsical giving her cord a playful twang.

"Ook," Calamity giving Lizzy's cord a heavier twang. Now alarmed with Calamity, her attitude towards Lizzy was changing. It was my fault, stupid monkey, but my thoughts clouded over, end of subject.

"No and it is very robust, or you did be a spirit already," I amazed at the cord's strength.

"Ook," someone does not like being described as a monkey going crazy showing me fangs dripping cobra venom, well, Calamity had imagination and full of the venom of jealous neglect.

So, bumped into my orb that made an illumination of light, which were noticeable as dark in the cabin and flight attendants saw, the pop musicians group saw, a mother taking the opportunity to catch up on her diary saw, and those with sleeping masks on did not.

THE PLANE WAS HAUNTED.

A flight attendant approached, stopped, went on, returned, Calamity always the joker misted an ape face. I heard an "Ook," the flight attendant muffled a scream, well trained, do not disturb first class passengers, but still wet her knickers. As she retreated an ape's giggles followed her to her friends who scattered. Well, being a plane scattered where?

THE PLANE WAS HAUNTED.

"By a monkey," a flight attendant was telling the navigator.

"Oh dear, sure she meant ape Calamity," Lizzy but our great ape was wiser, so terrified the whole plane.

The flight attendants screamed forgetting training shouting, "We are going to die?" The pop musicians swatted Calamity with expensive unpublished music sheets so would remain unpublished as ripped, the mother threw her diary and blackened a musician's eye, and those with sleeping masks took them off to put them back on, "we see, hear and touch nothing."

THE PLANE WAS HAUNTED, well-done ape, my dearest Calamity.

So, feet and toes painfully trampled, throats red from shouting abuse at anyone listening, plastic coffee cups thrown and rolled up magazines making a painful whacking sound in directions an ape ghost seen.

"Ouch," "Stop it fool," "my cosmetic nose," "what you whack me there for?" Heard.

I misted out of curiosity, well, ghosts stick together, Calamity needed reined in, yes, and was to chat with her when, "Henry," it was a warning to behave, well someone wears the trousers, and is not me, got no legs unless think them.

Pain killers never did anything for a ghost, it was a bible and praying, ghosts were not demons with fangs, but like us, your dead; dads, mums, siblings, pets, and okay, few were demons but existed before my time?

"Ook," Calamity showing demonic fangs being funny.

Now, I heard physicals say demons do not exist, well, you do not want to meet one.

Tell you this for free, lot of demons pretend to be a little girl child roaming your house, get you relaxed before becoming Dracula Unlimited?

But: "Back to hell demons," told you, as passengers threw religion at us two, but we were not demons, (well a monkey,) but orbs of Light.

"Ook," Calamity furious over 'monkey,' so her face became snarls in an orb directed towards me, but the humans thought it was to them, so panicked over a rabid Spider Monkey.

"Gasp," I breathed for air as Calamity throttled me, "Ook," which translated is, "spider monkey is it?"

"Behave you two," was Lizzy in our minds.

"Ook," Calamity shrinking away dreaming of figs, myself I went into Lizzy's mind thinking of Lizzy in swimwear on Bondi beach, my way of disarming the female threat by changing the subject.

"You perv out," Lizzy's reply so the female threat intensified.

But I took her there, leaving her physical body behind, and that is one of the benefits of having a ghost boy- friend.

"Ook," Calamity agreeing, and I and Lizzy were gone, now Calamity was annoyed as left behind, "God help the passengers."

"Is she dead?" One flight attendant asked the other as Lizzy was in deep mediation.

"Thank goodness, peace then?" An unnamed musician.

One of them returning with a vial she stuck up Lizzy's nose, a pong wake-up essence, Vicks Fisherman's Friend Extra Strong Lozenges. (Strong enough to make a zombie out of you.)

"Ook," Calamity misting in a large white orb, oh the cheeky playful ape, deliberately looking like a blown-up brown monkey and was out of proportion and ugly stinker.

There were gasps of air and screams as passengers fought each other to open the exit doors at thirty thousand feet.

There was a loud gasp for air as Lizzy rudely awoke.

I had associated with Calamity to long, thrown ripe melons at each other, "Ook," yes blame the ape and never me.

"Calamity get them away from the exit doors, dear, dearest ape," showing Calamity I had time for her. It worked, Calamity stopped herding passengers to the exit doors, the plane now at twenty-five thousand feet.

"Henry what a child you are? Are you always this playful?" Lizzy and did those words have a double meaning.

"Ook," Calamity chasing the stewardesses into the cockpit, but she had cleared the doors, "GOOD APE, hear me, GOOD APE."

Suddenly the plane lurched, then settled as autopilot took over.

On the intercom accidently switched on, see Calamity is an ape, has no idea what switches are, so all classes heard, "It is a real ghost, what does it want, to fly the plane, we are all dead?" The trembling pilot.

Well, everyone panicked, even Lizzy who saw Calamity crashing the plane.

"Do something Henry, now," oh well, a woman is really the boss in any relationship. I only helped as Lizzy called me 'Henry.'

"Another ghost," heard as I entered and took away Calamity telling her she could say hello to everyone aboard by coming with me.

"Henry, come back here with Calam," Lizzy, and suddenly Calamity became Calam, like a calm on the seabed.

"Ook," Calamity likening the closeness between her and Lizzy by the shortening of the name implied.

"Pt," for me and the passengers.

"God help us," "What a stink," "Open a window," "What do ghosts eat?"

Then laughter started and is infectious, so the plane became a jolly airplane at sixteen thousand feet.

"What are you idiots doing, we are waiting to infect these people," it was those spirits attached to passengers, for mostly those with bad intentions now building up in front of us, so the plane quietened; people knew what a dark orb meant, DEMON as looked at our orbs, which were white, we were the nice ghosts.

"People, the two ghosts you saw are Henry and his ape Calamity, they are good spirits and there are others like them here, they will help you rid the plane of these," Lizzy pointing at the dark orbs who rightfully took offence making sulphury stenches and raspberry sounds.

Orders are orders especially if you want the girl, so, was over in a matter of minutes, a light show, as white orbs pushed into the dark orbs, and dark hates light so, curled and snarled and fled into the starry Ether outside the jolly plane full of "three cheers for the ape," "hip hurray, the ape ghost saved us," "what is the ape's side kick called?" "The ape needs a slick hero outfit," "Don't forget the mask."

Yes, jolly as the passengers and crew where grateful Calamity had rid them of DEMONS.

Let them see them as DEMONS, it would take too long to explain using Lizzy's mouth, who I wanted all to myself, I was selfish, Lizzy was hot stuff, that the dark spirits were bad, not imps or demons.

"Ook," Calam agreeing, where did she come from, had I not left her getting adored.

"Henry," it was curt so reined in.

The plane flew on with Lizzy giving a lecture on the After Life so many believed and joyed singing   made-up hymns, prayers of thanks, and the flight attendants busy with noisy alcohol orders. Yes, the plane upgraded from jolly to merry.

At ten thousand feet the plane upgraded to drunken and what goes with too much alcohol, leering, pinching, secret rendezvousing, jealous Steve types planning murder.

*

In the cargo hold of another plane boxes of Borneo's artifacts, clubs used to bash an enemy to pulp, and shrunken heads, beads and stuffed animals and birds, venomous snake in preservative, shark teeth necklaces for the museum shop, all going to an exhibition in New York.

All infected with mischievous spirits, one being their leader, Roger DeJong. He had gone to the lower levels of darkness were cities existed, just as they do in the levels of Light. The Dark is a mirror of The Light, both existing in Heaven, the throbbing Mind?

Here Roger had pleaded with the Leader of Lies to let his friends accompany him to the physical plane for murderous intentions.

Well, they needed a holiday from Hell, so why had possessed artifacts that were travelling to a museum in New York; a base to foray to sample the delights of that city, Hot Dogs, Hamburgers, Drug Addicts, Prostitutes, Gangs, and the movie 'Twins.'

Any demons amongst them, Roger who was well on his way to becoming one.

*Figure 6 A street artist painting Sea Front
Hotel, Sandakan, 1921, cost US$1.*

Peter now recovered from malaria, sat in a rattan chair on the long veranda of the Sea Front Hotel in Sandakan. His hunchback in rags at his feet crunching on a crocodile bone, ha, it was Steve and he sat opposite Peter, silent, having learned to fear his new master, not exactly in rags but in need of a change of clothing style, still in an adventurer's army green outfit with tattered hat dangling fly corks.

He was not gnawing a bone but sipping The Tarik, condensed milk tea drink, rotting his teeth with sugar, but he was addicted, and on a side plate yes gnawed remains of Umai, the dish for a sweltering day, and is always hot in Borneo. The fried mackerel was in Steve along with the added calamansi limes. Strange sounds and silent smells emitted from Steve who put on an angelic face and pointed at the parrot on a bird stand.

He was still an imported person and not spent a lifetime allowing his innards time to absorb spicy foods.

Luckily there where toilets nearby and Steve could sprint when needed.

He was slowly becoming obese as he just spent his time eating silently opposite Peter, wondering how he got into this mess; soon the rich meal did make more rude noises and produce silent stinkers.

"I hate her," and blamed Lizzy instead of himself. She had deliberately led him to believe she wanted him. Steve knew what he did do to her when Peter gave her to him. Start feeding her all this condensed milk food and watch her teeth decay as he watched his. Anyone did think he was a drug addict, and he swallowed a quinine tablet against malaria.

"Yes, do that Steve," a voice in his right temple begged, it belonged to a shadowy male figure that never materialized in Steve's mind, or he did die of fright and Lizzy did be safe, ha. Instead, sometimes would appear peeking round a wall corner at Steve, who would blink and deliberately dismiss what he had seen as imagination, but we ghosts know better, it was a **shadow spirit.**

To admit seeing the shadow person would be admitting he was in the wrong company and possessed by evil, wake up, blame himself, not Lizzy or Henry, which he could never do as was comfortably weak never being wrong crunching up delicious insects and drinking condensed milk tea. In his pocket a crumpled picture of an ape, he did have to stop producing it and whispering, "I hate you," just in case people watching him thought he was insane.

He did not have to pay for these delicacies, it went on Peter's tab. Even the bedroom was free, that included employees, and he showed these what he did do to Lizzy so earned himself a deserved reputation?

'**The insect man,**' as even starker's insect chitin legs stuck out of his mouth.

"**Boy with rotten teeth and small whatever,**" as Steve was not only obese but needing insulin.

"**Big European man Here,**" and was an insult as Steve was the opposite.

"**Aroma here,**" as the girls tried to entice Steve into a bath, full of scalding water to be rid of him, as hated his mysterious ways. They say, "He was chasing a roach, slipped on soap and fell in."

"Big tipper," as never tipped so Steven was loathed.

"Nuttery Steve and his monkey friend," that was invisible but was the shadow person advising him on matrimonial affairs under an overhead electric fan.

The shadow person did not want Steve to become uncomfortable or did have to leave. One day it would take Steve's soul to where it was heading, to an Outer Darkness that was thick enough not to be able to see your spirit body; but hear the wailing and gnashing of teeth Steve lookalikes by the dozen.

A luscious juicy roach went by heading for the dark safety underneath Steve's rattan cushioned chair.

 From a roof rafter of the hotel a pet Rehearse monkey dropped and gobbled up the roach.

"Lovely," silently thought as it wiped fingers, "full of vitamin E."

Peter saw a caricature of himself in the monkey so lashed out a left foot and missed, but kicked Steve, which was all right, Steve disgusted him as yes, he saw himself in Steve, selfish, cruel, materialistic, and womanizing, but not the insect eating part.

"Gawd," Steve screamed as the little cute monkey bit him, no imbecile tried to kick her.

The shadow person appeared gloating over the bite. The shadow person knew it did have to teach Steve what to do with those employees through possession that called him names; and was looking forward to getting away from sugary condensed teas to drugs, alcohol, and axes.

"No, go away, you don't exist," Steve moaned as the shadow patted his head and vanished. Now Steve felt a coldness flow down his spine to his privates, so badly, that he reached down to feel they were alive and a few minutes searching under belly rolls, found them.

As for the monkey it cleared off through an open window into the jungle, laughing.

Steve needed a tetanus and rabies jab, but he was too lazy to see about it. Instead, he wheezed his way to the hotel for first aid that was a band aid on the small bite.

Am I saying the monkey had rabies, no, who knows, let us say a hungry leopard hanging about dark streets waiting for inumbrated folks to eat, ate it?

So, who knows if Mr. Monkey had rabies?

Did it manage to bite the leopard who did spread it about local drunkards?

Peter looked at Steve, he was disgusted, the man needed to lose weight if he was to serve him, so, clicking fingers and hotel female workers quickly arrived, Peter gave them instructions, their faces illuminated with joy and went to push Steve into the dark corridors behind the reception desk.

"Leave me alone, I work for Peter," he pleaded.

"We work for Peter too," and giggled the girls replied shoving him down a laundry chute, it was dark down there, the girls thought a week without food would lose Steve a few pounds, and one tucked the key to the basement in her knickers. Nope, these hotel female workers were them that called Steve horrid names and forgot roaches roamed the basement as the rats were fat down there.

So, when Steve appeared one month later in tiger striped 'Y' Fronts as a stuffed conversation piece on the wall above the reception, he had lost weight, the rats were greedy and never shared a single roach with him.

"Make the fat boy lose weight pronto," Peter had instructed.

Just why was Steve on the wall, he knew flying insects rested there, waiting till darkness to do nightly routines like biting you.

He was starving, the only way to get him down was to put a roach in a jar and shake, "Come along Freddy," a girl knowing his name was Steve, and so got Steve down.

*

Peter sat in first class enjoying life, flight attendants to ogle and feed him food.

He was on his way to New York, which was what the post card from Uncle Roger said, 'Get here quick or else join me.'

Peter understood, the 'join me' part was a death threat.

He also knew who was boss of this operation, Peter. So, why was he obeying, he was afraid of boogiemen. Since he could not ask for religious local help, he relied on colored stones that grinded, crunched and silently ripped away his expensive silk pockets of his tartan suits.

Peter had seen millions of American tourists, they all wore tartan, so would he, that explains why he was in a yellow and black Buchan tartan.

Yes, Peter stuck out like the yellow flowering Buchan plant the tartan took after, for camouflage when clan law did not exist in Scotland, when Peter replicas roamed the roads seeking vulnerable folks on the way home, such as dandy Nobles in coaches protected by bribed coachmen to run away when trouble flared, the Steve's and ate insects back then too.

Pensioner couples away to see their grandchildren for the first and last time, as a Peter replica got them, took their clothes, even wooden shoes, canes and left them nothing.

"Howl," hungry wolves.

And Peter played the part of a New York Art dealer trying to impress the flight attendant into his hotel room later.

"I am an Art Dealer also, I am Steve, Hawkins, you are?" A touring Americano said over him. At the name Steve, Peter choked on an olive in his martini. No, it was not Steve come back to haunt him as a bogeyman, his Steve was alive, chained in a box in the cargo hold in his new clothes.

Tranquilized to keep him asleep and away from Peter till they met up with Roger DeJong again.

Steve Hawkins sat done next to Peter and talked shop, his voice attracting the other first class passenger's attention, the plane movie a documentary on John Lennon and the Beetles, unfortunately these first-class travelers where 'Who' fans.

"Hey, what sort of Art dealer are you?" Steve Hawkins asked when Peter gave the wrong answers to Steve Hawkins questions.

It was time to get rid of this man as Peter knew nothing about art.

How did he get rid of Steve Hawkins?

Peter noticed the man's tie and socks were pink and he had been drinking.

Peter concluded the man was gay so winked and parted a lip exposing bit of tongue. He would entice the man to the bathroom and punch him in the throat, ends of story.

"Excuse me honey," Peter forced himself to say knowing this disposal job was a job for Steve, where was that imbecile, then remembered he was in the cargo hold in his new clothes.

As Peter squeezed by, he squeezed part of the man and giggled and as a flight attendant approached, said in a deep voice, "Excuse me mate, need the loo."

"It is alright, our airline is gender friendly Mr. Jong," the flight attendant, to Peter, 'the bl8888 woman just told this sh88 my name and looped down the plane interior using passing seat head rests as handrails, catching hair, causing screams, squashing fingers, breaking old arthritic bones, but he got to the loo.

"Who the hell does that creep think he is?" Steve Hawkins whispered, and the flight attendant needing a hearing aid, "Oh he said was going to the loo."

Steve Hawkins followed.

He was one of these men that wore flattened gold rings on his fingers as a D.I.Y. knuckle duster and get away with it.

His ears pierced, and the sides of his nose, and he liked pink, and his gold casual shirts were pink.

He liked his women in pink too.

Did I neglect to say he liked his men in pink, he did not like men in anything but men stuff.

He knocked on the loo door Peter was behind.

Behind that door Peter was ready to maneuver Steve into a receiving punch position.

"There is no room for a hamster in this stinking loo," Peter cursed changing to Plan B, trouble was there was no plan B.

Steve knocked again, panic gripped Peter flight attendants did be attracted to the knocking, as said, 'This is a gender friendly airline.'

Peter opened the door.

"Alcoholic breath enveloped him, blurring his vision, choking him, making him wretch so was not fair he never got to:

Drag Steve Hawkins into the loo by the throat, nails digging into arteries. Any bloodstained clothes Peter did stuff down the plane loo, obviously never used a plane loo.

Poke any Steve resistance away with pokes to the eyes with fingers.

Knee the wind out of Steve Hawkins by repeatedly kneeing him man places.

Ripping Steve's pink tie off and garroting Steve with a bar of soap between the tie and flesh.

Undoing Steve's belt so his grey tartan trousers did fall to his ankles hindering a counterattack.

Take Steve's real alligator shoes as had white caps whereas Peter's were P.V.C. fake crocodile shoes as shined up better, did not want to make the fellow passengers think he was a cheap stake.

Never got to rip off those hated pink socks and wonder what to do with them and had a brain wave from a dark imp giving advice on a shoulder, which explains why Steve pulled away Steve's dark tartan trousers and stuffed the hated pink socks somewhere.

But all this never happened because of Steve's alcoholic breath breathed upon him; just as a flight attendant passed giggling over them, and to help them with these words, "Our Airline is gender friendly," pushed Steve Hawkins into the loo and shut the door. His uncovered mouth closed upon Pete's who inhaling deeply in no time was drunk, so never felt Steve, pound him with massive fists that had D.I.Y. knuckle dusters.

Knee him repeatedly man places making sure Peter did be useless in an Airline practicing gender equality.

Stick Peter's head down the loo and flush, and like other airplanes, did not work, so Peter ended up stinking of what Jesus said, "Do not be alarmed, what you eat comes out as waste," a natural process, or said something akin.

With someone else's loo paper in his mouth, Peter tried to spit out but found his mouth stretched by massive hands and his tongue pulled out to his feet, then wrapped about a hot water tap left on.

At least Peter undressed by Steve would not get cold.

And since Peter did not have pink socks, Steve stuck his P.V.C. shoes places, then took photos on his mobile phone, those cameras tyrants hate.

And left leaving the restroom door ajar.

Soon a passing flight attendant remarked to her friends, "These gay people play rough games," and shut and locked the door and put a red OUT OF ORDER sign on the door.

Just as well Peter studied all the 'Wild Toad' moves of Jackie Chan, and the Slap a Mosquito' moves of Bruce Lee, as needed a Houdini mind to free himself.

"Listen to him, he cannot get enough, disgusting," passing flight attendants no longer passing but using clear glasses to listen into Peter's agonizing efforts to untangle the knots Steve put him in.

Lucky for Peter he was triple jointed and for Steve or the flight attendants did twig foul play was a foot and security called.

"I am free, what is this stuck to my lips," and Peter peeled off loo paper, used condoms, other thingamabobs unmentionable but imaginable, a baby poisonous salamander flushed away as customs did fine the owner $10,000 for breaching immigration rules.

"I am dying," Peter as the poisonous salamander chewed his left pinkie, never minds that allowed him to use his right hand and open the loo door and collapse into the arms of flight attendants, who did not want Peter in their arms, especially with a strange newt type creature hopping about them, chewing each in turn.

And Peter fell atop the newt type creature that began chewing his tummy, thinking escape by coming out the back of Peter.

And three flight attendants chewed by the newt fell atop Peter and whose combined weight squashed the poisonous salamander, thus saving Peter's life.

Look, a white mist leaving the poisonous salamander as it went upwards to The Light, deer ahead in a queue scattered, it was still a poisonous salamander.

*

"That is the last screw undone using my tongue," the real

Steve in the cargo hold of the plane, "FREEDOM," he screamed thinking he was alone.

"Woof," "hiss," "meow," came replies.

"Oh, creatures to eat, oh sorry, creatures to be friends with," Steve thinking insect as there was no flight attendant service in the cargo hold.

Now hunger does strange things to a mind, especially a twisted mind, as Steve freed ten strange looking dogs, 'WOLVER-INES' was on their cages. He delighted in seeing them as giant dung beetles as stuck in cages for a long time, well, nature wins, and might explain the hanging lump in Steve's pants.

"Oh, sweet kitties," and freed ten strange looking cats, "Highland Wild Cats," was on a sign above their cage.

"Hiss," Steve not freeing these creatures as they rattled.

The last had 'Indonesian Hobbit' above their box, sealed so no one could peek in.

"You are all free except them," pointing at the rattlers, and Steve wanted to eat them all, as imagined them all as tasty Dung beetles, except the hobbits who looked like tiny men and women wearing fig leaves.

These he began to realize might come in handy since they were worshipping him as an idol, "He has freed us, he is our god now," the tiny hobbits from Indonesia.

Then the hungry wolverines decided to eat the wild cats who knew all about wolverines back home. They were just drunken farmers in fur looking for fairies in silver birch woods, as could sell them to tourists, but were so drunk were lost and the fairy tale seemed a story to tell the wife why they were in the woods, alone, and at the other ends of the woods, a real fairy drove away, oh yeh, tell us more?

"I must flee or be torn to bits by these thingmabobs," Steve not liking the odds as the fighting animals got closer to him, and that is when the lift opened and a flight attendant stood there, terrified is not the word.

Ten little hobbits ran in and pawed her to pieces as wanted to know what a human woman was, and that lecherous Steve followed and did not help the flight attendant who pleaded with him, "Help me."

"Why?" He asked as was a mentally deranged insect eater.

So, do not worry help was coming to the flight attendant as a hobbit pressed 'UP' so, the lift went up and opened.

Screams filled topside as ten hobbits, ten wolverines, ten wild cats ram about the passengers.

"Sally you, ok?" a fellow flight attendant asked.

"Sure," sally replied seeking the loo to reflect upon life's recent adventure, and unlocked Peters.

"Master found you," Steve seeing Peter in an awkward position.

"Get me clothes," Peter ordered Steve but failed to gender them so, Steve went from passenger seat to seat ripping clothes of folks. Poor beaten up Peter made the mistake of letting his Igor, Steve dress him so the bra gave him a 46D chest, the corset no air to breath so winded him continually, the stiletto shoes blisters, and the red lipstick once the purple wig was on, the lips of Calamity.

Then the plane lurched as the auto pilot took the plane down in an emergency landing at New York. Down in the hold the box with the rattlers in thrashed and crashed against a wall, splintering, emptying a dozen nasty rattlers about.

Never mind, the rattler box also hit cargo door open button, so the nasty rattlers were sucked out the plane, sparing any pretty flight attendants a bite.

Do, not fret snake lovers, the plane was now down to a hundred feet and the dozen rattlers flew slithering on nothing.

Splash times twelve as they landed in a former Presidents swimming pool. Gold golf clubs and golf balls littered the pool side, as did blond wigs.

A luscious floozy sunbathed as the pool had infra-red lamps.

She had ear plugs in listening to replays of her husbands' speeches, so was asleep.

Just as well, for lovers of luscious girls sunbathing in bikinis, as movement attracts slithers who headed for the golf course and FREEDOM.

"Four," shouted down on the golf course as the former president missed a hole in one and bent his clubs about the caddie, an electric caddie, so relax, but needed to escape the ten rattlers attracted by his movements coming his way.

That ends the story of the rattlers, a happy one as free, but angry at travelling in boxes.

Now about the wolverines and wild cats, they mauled everything that moved, the pilots too explaining why the plane was on autopilot, so they were free for the clawing.

And Steve stood still, amazed by what he was watching, fleas shredded from the animals, waiting for one to get close, and then like lighting a hand shot out, catching the flea, and he was motionless again, except jaw movements.

Slowly his tummy extended, the only proof a hand had been active.

Then the plane landed and all those not with a seat belt flew.

"Look Peter, we are flying," Steve as they flew out an emergency exit that auto opened, and do not worry, not a bone broke, as the inflatable emergency shoot opened, and down they went into the waiting caring loving arms of an ambulance crew, whose mental state did never be the same again after this lift.

Oh yes, almost forgot, ten wolverines and ten wild cats came down the shoot and tumbled into the ambulance. Peter in drag shut the doors, afraid of recognition, you just never know, a Malayan fried mackerel vendor might have taken that flight to visit his cousins selling chili hot dogs on New York streets.

"The world is a small place Master," Steve grooming the animals for snacks.

*

Somewhere amongst the city streets the ambulance crew jettisoned the vehicle. The driver was the first to go as wolverines fought him for a turn at the steering wheel. I mean all he could see was furry bottoms, sharp small fangs, bushy tails slapping his face and smell wolverine Winds, "In heavens name, what do you creatures eat?"

For an answer five left the steering wheel and showed him, so he had a handful of wolverines trying to rip his throat and innards apart.

"I am out of here," he said, so hit the brake, well he and ten wolverines flattened against the windscreen. Never mind, be happy, the ten furry wolverines provided soft padding for his head hitting the windscreen.

Yes, "FREEDOM," he breathed loudly leaping from the stalled ambulance in front of a number 478 bus to the Bronx. Never mind first aid was at hand as his companion in the back, seeing his escape leapt from the back of the ambulance onto the road.

"FREEDOM," she gasped sneezing as was allergic to cat hair.

From the back of the stalled ambulance ten wild cats eyed her with disgust, "meow," they hissed, "come back here and finish the fight," the cats hissed but did not venture out as there Dog and Cat Wardens lurked to catch and make feline dumplings out of them, as some idiot called Steve had talked about his tummy yummies expanding to include 'Wolverine sausage accompanied by Wild Cat Dumplings in sage,' as Steve had imagination and the cats understanding his tummy rumbles, believed him.

Now as the ambulance driver's co-worker ran to his aid, the number 478 Bronx ran into her, as the driver was not stopping, afraid she would lose her bus license as had sixteen children to feed as lived in an unheated giant cardboard shoe billboard.

Right across the windscreen the female ambulance life saver flattened with these words, "Stop the bus please."

Well, the bus did stop as the bus driver went into a state of apoplectic shock, so the bus ran over ten red fire hydrants and stopped from an oil leak.

Water rained down everywhere, and the street filled with children, and the steps to apartment blocks with vest wearing folk chatting about the rigged presidential election.

"Drive Steve, get us away from here before the police arrive Peter's first sensible sentence of the whole story so far.

"Yes Steve, let me help you," was Roger DeJong levitating Steve into the driver's seat.

Both Steve and Roger had never driven in their life, so killers were at the wheel.

Furry types, ten Wolverines and ten nasty felines, for it says, "Hell knows no furry like a woman scorned," and since were so savage no one bothered to find out their gender.

So, that makes twelve fools driving with no knowledge of the Highway Code.

In the back a woman began to pray, oh it was Peter still in drag.

Figure 7 Steven looking for Peter and butterflies and roaches.

A certain vendor selling chili foods was on his way to the airport to greet a relative, being a model citizen with a clean police record, he pushed his wheeled kitchen onto the pedestrian crossing.

"I am not going down for Jay Walking, I know cops are hiding behind billboards advertising Clean Teeth Advertisements," and hummed a happy ditty, "This is America, I want a slice of the dream, the biggest cut, a red Cadillac, swimming pool and cocaine parties at the pool side to dope floozy girls up, for I is as ugly as sin, yes I am happy as sold two hundred chili hot dogs today and going to meet my cousin, and get him working for me on lies, lies that he will be sent home if he receives a pay, it must be voluntary work for ten years to apply for U.S.A. citizenship."

Yes, away in a dream world drooling over Dolly Patton, so, never heard the squabbling drivers, never heard the squill of tires, never smelt the rubber burn, but did look with one eye and see wolverines behind the wheel, ten felines at the wheel, Steve at the wheel, and a ghost, to him the 'Grim Reaper,' and said, "I do not think anyone is driving that ambulance come for me."

Yes, run over, a man with ambition, an extra so expendable. In the back somewhere a real ambulance crew on strike, so playing cards and drinking pints of black coffee without sugar, the

American way.

And Steve was hungry with all this exercise, so took from a pocket a packet of dried earwigs, fried in lemon grass, which he did never get through custom as was lethal to American earwig breeders who bred them to sell lizard pet owners a dinner, Steve's had disease. Germs that fermented the innards so explains about Steve's bad gas.

So, the ten wolverines and ten felines stopped fighting and looked at Steve who stared back.

This was his snack, they could 'b88888 off', but their stares became slits of hate and their mouths opened showing fangs dripping tetanus ridden saliva.

"Just throw the blooming snack out the window," a whisper and was Peter behind him fed up with living. Fed up with living as did not specify which window, so Steve through the earwig snack through the partition window at Peter.

Immediately Steve was alone driving with an admiring Roger DeJong who thought, "If only Peter was like you."

Because it was so noisy with Peter screaming making new friends, Steve closed the partition window to concentrate on driving.

"We are going to a museum, you can live in the dump of a hotel across the road where poor immigrants are supposed to live, thus not drawing attention to yourselves," Roger to Steve. A pity he did not speak to Steve's mind or did find Steve was not listening but thinking of where he put an emergency snack, and remembered, a pressed dried centipede in his shoe.

By chance, The Rothschild Museum of Anthropology came into view as Steve struggled for a shoe, but which foot hid his snack.

Roger saw his holiday homer appear and disappear as Steve drove past, took a sharp right and smashed through the museum basement gates.

"The disappointment of passing the museum faded, replaced by hero worship from Roger.

"Take Peter across the street and stay low in the hotel, you are expected, I have friends in New York," Roger.

Steve nodded vigorously, Roger was impressed more, Roger loved 'Yes' men, they obeyed.

As Steve took Peter by the hand, out of the museum basement he spat out the living centipede and stopped nodding. He did never buy 'Wong's Singapore Insect Surprise Treat, 'again.

Peter tried to shake free,

"Hey this is our territory girl," two gender friendly night workers approaching Peter.

"What, no you misunderstand, I am Peter," but he could call himself 'Handsome Prince Charming,' they still would rob, beat, steal his clothes, especially the stilettos and leave him in his lingerie's, as night workers were hygienic and did not wear another's unmentionables.

And Steve went off behind the bushes with these two-night workers and the question are?

Did Steve have rabies from a monkey eaten by a leopard?

He had malaria from a mosquito but all the insects he ate were full of quinin, so cured him, but left him a carrier of Yellow Fever.

The fleas he ate gave him typhus and the plague.

Because he never bathed, he had cholera and other nasty germs.

"Here is that an insect in your mouth?" One of the nightworkers soon admitted to emergency.

"I am coming out in smelly black carbuncles?" The other night-worker on her way to the morgue as both were extras and would act in any scene for a stardom break.

So, Steve pulled up his rotten unmentionables and picked up all the stolen wallets, Peter's cash, that the two-night workers had dropped to empty insects from their pockets and handbags, for Steve had escaped bugs hiding on him now on them, the biting variety such as that centipede he had kept in a shoe.

"Humpy Dumpty sat on a wall," Steve sang skipping to the hotel.

"I sent the night worker to your room, said his name was Peter," and "can I sell you any of this?" The hotel check in attendant and from hidden swivel drawers' items of sadism to use on Peter.

Steve bought the lot using his newfound wealth.

"Hey, no pets," the hotel clerk watching ten wolverines and ten felines run past Steve and up the stairwell, just as well the Indonesian Hobbits were stuck at immigration as had no passports.

"Not mine," Steve telling the truth as he had not adopted them as pets.

Anyway, outside Peter's door, Peter swore he heard panting, as it was a long run up twenty-one flights of stairs, even for animals.

"Must be Steve, I will beat him, kick him, bite him, throttle him, strip him naked and put down the loo his insects," Peter and laughed.

"What are you laughing for, you have done nothing while poor Steve has done all the work, pull your stockings up or I finish with you," the warning came from the ghost of Roger DeJong who had travelled across the street from the museum to be here.

From a window glass panel, a face of a misted-up ape.

Behind the ape a breathing ghost misting the glass pane, me.

"Ook," I cannot see a thing.

"I smell the blood of an English ape," Roger DeJong sniffing the air. Then the door burst open as Steve entered followed by the adopted pets and loved Peter so much hugged him black and blue.

"Master where art thou," Steve not able to see Peter for he was now furry. "Oh, we are playing YETI, GOODIE," AND AN IDIOT CLAPPED HIS HANDS AND HUGGED Peter and all the animals in that hug fainted from Steve's stink.

"Peace at last," Peter passing out too.

Therefore, Roger forgot us at the misted glass windowpane, he was possessing Peter to wake up, check the wardrobes for any left male clothes, and wipe off the red lipstick.

Peter found a discarded Scout Uniform and with a sigh dressed.

"I know where Lizzy is Peter, as soon as Henry and the monkey leave to buy monkey nuts, we can visit, repeat Peter what can we do?" Now Roger had used 'monkey' twice as he smelt the blood of an English ape nearby, and 'monkey' used to flush Calamity out.

"Ook," Calamity drifting through the glass and squaring off with Roger, there were ten wolverines and ten felines looking at her, forcing Calamity to smarten up. She knew love on our Spirit side knew no boundaries, and if I could hold Lizzy, Calamity could hope for romance with them.

"Attack," Roger commanded the pets, but they did not, animals stick together.

Yes Master," Steve lumbering forward, standing on tails so was ripped to shreds.

"What bravery," Roger, "if only Peter was like that," and vanished back to his museum.

What did Peter do, he watched and laughed, found sour milk in the fridge, a packet of digestives, a chewed chocolate bar and a bottle of a famous diet canned drink, and ate the digestives, gargled with the sour milk, wrote his will with the chocolate bar on a wall, and opened the fizzy drink tin that should have brought the pets to him, but they did not, why, had Jesus answered his prayer?

No, the pets lay exhausted, he gave the sour milk to Steve.

"Thank you Master, now I know you love me," Steve.

In another hotel Lizzy received a mobile phone call, "Hello, whose there?"

"Fax," the reply.

"Fax," Lizzy alarmed, excited and horrified.

*

Back with Lizzy, "Roger is living in a museum, Peter I never knew, is a gender issue, and they are planning to steal the bones,"

I told Lizzy, when she was a target also, but that had slipped my ghost mind over seeing Peter in drag.

"Fancy him, do we?" Lizzy asked.

"Ook," Calamity forgetting also Lizzy was a target, as she was in love with many pets and dreaming of husbands and funny looking offspring. I did not have the heart to tell her they were physical husbands, and she was a ghost, there would be no children, but who knows?

"I believe we are safe tonight, a rest would be nice," but Lizzy seemed to be in a different world. I snooped about an open living room drawer she had been in, lot of photos of men, family, more men, zoo animals, more men, men, men, men. Why had she made that cruel humorless remark about drag and me?

The drawer closed, "Henry," it was a warning to stay out. I entered her head, "Honey, it is me."

"I know," and that was that she went off to eat dinner alone, a quick television meatless meal. I tried entering again, her mind had blocked me out, but noticed she murmured fondly a name, 'Fax.'

"Fax who?" I asked loudly, jealousy aroused.

"A friend," Lizzy said patting my mist.

A landline rang, Lizzy answered, and talked to a reporter about Ramapithecus. A news team did be over soonest as Lizzy knew once aired, Roger could no longer hide in the shadows.

And just where was Roger?

I drifted away from Lizzy, hurt, "Coming Calamity?"

"Ook," Calamity dreaming of romantic meetings with pets.

And drifted away to a museum that from the outside was darker than the night. It shouted, "Dark entities are here," and for effect I heard howling so shivered in my orb.

"Hail Roger Caesar," I heard the dark entities cheer so had a look, and to my horror through a misted windowpane saw Roger, standing atop a dinosaur head waving to those cheering.

Dark creatures The Lord had made, creatures with humanoid bodies and animal heads, hence the howling. I felt sorry for them as I had a creature too called Calamity and looked about for her fearing for my life. Had I got away with my Calamity joke, or had I not?

CH8 NEW HOME

Figure 8 Bull shark lives in fresh and salt water, so beware skimpy dippers, especially the Melbourne freshwater canals. Yeh, let your four-year-old's safely splash about in rubber tubing.

With Peter awake, Roger DeJong admired his homely new museum surroundings. My, there was gold, brass, and mummified servants at hand.

Roger sat in a Byzantine emerald embedded throne, no doubt the corrupt Emperor Justinian who people said when bowing to him, in whispers of course, we see demon advisors next to him, where are the human ones?" "Look the lions are fat," the reply. "Where is God?" "In both," a reply.

So, Roger puffed and drank Egyptian beer pored to him by pharaohs.

A barbarian ghost queen combed his hair for nits.

The building was full of the dead. The mummified hands and mummies of ordinary people did not greet Roger, they had not been evil people during their lives, just people with ancient ways of living such as mummifying cats and Time Travelers.

The spirits of the animals grouped about the different museum floor level railings not trusting Roger. Creatures of Spirit and now prisoners of Roger and his dark entity friends. They needed a leader, whom would it be?

"Oh, Calam where art thou, figs in it," she might, does anything for figs?

From Roger's spirit oozed the cries of creatures he had hunted for cash.

Roger to them was an executioner, a murderer, avoided even in death for the Grim Reaper was his doppelganger, Roger's ghostly double.

The dinosaur framed skeletons, their spirits were strong and mighty, but had no need for food in the After Life so Roger and company were safe from a spirit fight.

Can spirits fight, ask the Tyrannosaurus dinosaur, the museum called him 'Freddy.'

Roger and company tried to put the museum into darkness, by flooding it with dark energy, but the good spirits here objected, and a firework of orbital Light occurred, and Freddy was good, Freddy knew children played with his felt toys and loved him, why they stuffed the toys full of crisps, peanuts and chewing gum, and Freddy loved the children back as their energy fed him.

Drivers, dog walkers, passing patrol car occupants, prostitutes on the corners and drug addicts and others in the bushy evergreen shrubs noticed this supernatural event and Freddy's giant shadow cast high through museum windows to the stars.

"Always said the place was hunted," one of the security guards.

"Agreed," a night-worker distracted zipping up a client's zipper and the night filled with a scream of agony.

"Wow," a drug addict in the next bush squirting his load into the air, so mesmerized was he by the colored orbs battling it out, "Sh88", I crawled under a moving bus as a dare to get my cash for that load," and explains the tire marks on his body.

"It is Jesus, I will become a nun," a lover pushing off her boyfriend.

"Nawa, aliens," and pulled her back to him, so she beat him up.

A passing patrol car drove over the lot as the police officer's inside were staring at Freddy's shadow.

A male pedestrian wrapped about the front patrol bumpers put his chiwahwa onto the bonnet and said, "I am suing."

An officer inside responded by pulling the open bonnet plug. "Whack," the rising bonnet hitting the dog walker, his head about to crash into the road and obliterate his skull, but he was close to the bushes and his head bounced safely off the lovers.

"Sexual pervert," the lovers so beat him with a brasserie and a 'Y' Front bleached for stiffness, socks were softer but still worn.

"Jesus Christ save me, and I will not sue but give 10% of my pension to the police charity pension fund," what a prayer and the lovers tired so left him alone, and the lovers collapsed back into their cuddling.

And the man went to look for his dog, the chihuahua peeing on the patrol car bonnet, it snarled at the officers inside and then ran into the bushes to bite a drug addict as the dog knew police officers were tough and addicts weak from overdoses, so was a safer bet.

And because the man had no intention of honoring his prayer to Jesus, the weak addict said, "This you 'F' dog, and stuck a syringe full of L.S.D. and addict blood into the man who was last seen running about naked catching imaginary hares, hedgehogs, hogs and girls, so the police officers shot him, he, he was an extra who was acting strangely in the hope of more pay.

"Honor your prayers," a voice from the Ether whispered as always does so never listened to.

The disgruntled client of the prostitute jumped out of the bushes waving his arms, screaming obscenities at the night. His zipper was still open, unfortunately.

"It is huge," a police officer noticing him.

"It is a flesh-eating worm, hey the dude is heading this way," the second officer pulling out his gun, any excuse, these where descendant of Wild Bill and Sundance, the mentality that is, and both fired a hundred bullets at the Mannie jumping about with the open zipper and missed as although an extra was acting his part, not like the dog owner, and was not his dog anyway but the stories.

And because the zipper owner jumped about not a bullet hit him, but hit an electric substation making sparks, putting the Bronx into darkness.

*

It was nearby the museum; the zoo Lizzy took our company.

Calamity was so excited over the other primates, male apes,

we left her to be apish and find romance. To make sure she carried a sack of real figs, "Love bought was the same as love not bought, it was love," Calamity with an "Ook."

"What will you do with the canvas bags?" I asked Lizzy.

"I had the press come round, they were on television," Lizzy replied.

"Wont this alert, Roger?" I asked.

"We can manage the dirty spook," she replied and what a lady; I overflowed with want, so thought a light off and door locked.

"Hey, put the light on," Lizzy had work to do, she wanted to lay out the contents of the bags. She had declared them at customs and the press knew. Pretty soon the phone would ring, and Lizzy did organize times and days; I was forgotten, how, I am a ghost called Henry; and ignored human ways.

"Ook," Calamity siding with Lizzy with an empty bag.

"Going on television again Henry, what can Roger do now, it will be too late?" She asked.

What would a bad ghost like him do? Well, what would I do in his place, destroy the bones out of nastiness, get Peter to kidnap Lizzy, sell her to a madam, worse give her to Steve??

"Go watch Peter?" Lizzy reading my thoughts, "is he dead?"

This was a command to me and Calamity to find out. Yes, taking Calamity as where Peter is would need help.

"Want you back later for dinner?" Lizzy playing with a light switch. That galvanized me, I was off seeking Calamity and from there find a portal to enter SPIRIT. It did be easier to enter the front door, via the greeting LIGHT when you die, but the swirling energy there can entrap you.

Better to find a portal and be sneaky, come and go at will.

Such the rigors of being a ghost in love.

"Woof," I woofed as misted next to Calamity in the gorilla house.

"He is certainly huge," I whispered to my friend.

"Ook," Calamity loudly so the gorillas looked at me thoughtfully, if only I was physical, it did rip me up so band aids would be useless.

So, gorillas watched Calamity go with resignation, holding up five fingered palms in the universal peace sign, but gorillas instead sent violent thoughts to me that messed me.

Remember animals see spirit, bold enough to say can project their living gorilla thought into a ghost, me and why I am so black and blue as did not like humans, even human ghosts, humans had stuck them in a cage with no privacy, why when they needed a 'dump' a hundred humans flashed them with cameras.

Sure, heard Calamity "Ook," which means "you rejected me," as to why she let her boys beat the living s**t out of me.

Then dark shadow spies alerted Roger to our squabbling.

"I cannot resist this, I am coming," Roger and sent a secret message to Peter playing Play Station, totally addicted; so, secret you cannot be told, even I do not know.

Then we were gone, and the gorillas thinking, happy banana thoughts as no longer feared death or me, they had seen spirits so knew that waited for them after death. So, danced, threw bananas against the compound wall, rattled the cages wakening up every living creature, for they were celebrating.

And we two, Calamity and me where in the Ether.

"What are you wearing?" I asked Calamity realizing she was in a brown furry Super one-piece stretch outfit, with mask. A smiling ape face was across the chest.

"Ook," and "pt.," then the universal finger.

*

We passed a sign, 'level one paradise,' and stopped at 'three,' here sought De Jong's family records for his weaknesses.

It was a failure as although I entered the Hall of Records, his deceased family members had other ideas. Like rabbits outnumbered us by a hundred to two and drove us back into level one.

Above we heard trumpets, angels coming to sort out De Jong's brood.

"Ook," Calamity suggesting to the angels they give them to Demonics, who did treat them kindly by boiling them in larva. I never had an evil thought towards them even as I knew them as Robbers of The After Life, all were kindred spirits.

"Ook," I will not translate Calame's thoughts, but she threw rotten fruits suggesting I was a hypocrite.

As we were busy never figured Dr Jong was entering Peter's head, the latter having played Mine Craft for the last ten hours and was now brain dead.

In the hotel lounge corner hunched on the carpet, Steve, who passed time by investigating the worn carpet, already needing replaced as covered in drug, blood, and other imagination spillage.

Did this man ever get those tetanus, rabid shots in Sandakan, well now he needed penicillin added.

"Lizzy alone did you say?" Peter.

"Yes," Roger fed up repeating the answer so possessed making a zombie of Peter. A lone brave prostitute in another corner finally became alarmed, it was the were-wolf howl Peter emitted plus leaping on Steve hoping for a leg, as Roger had filled him with blood lust, forgetting to point Peter towards Lizzy.

Steve was a monster Igor, obedient even till the bonfires so Roger happily patted Peter until the later humped his ghost orb.

Oh well, Roger went insane and threw Peter out an open window, so he thumped his way down a metal fire escape, knocking off the ladder ten meowing cats, six rose pots, twenty weed pots, a romantic couple and thirteen addicts too busy playing with needles to notice their descent to the parked cars below.

"What have I done?" Roger asked himself, a natural question after murdering someone, but the dark shadow spirits fearing Roger's wrath and The King of Lies for not saving Peter, caught him. The medium Douglas Holmes rubbed his face in hot coals, Saint John was boiled in hot oil, and not a burn, **Spirit when bothered**, can save you.

The splat marks on the pavement were the thirteen addicts.

The rough sleepers running away had picked up the fallen addicts' drugs so would be in Happy Land, where they did feel no cold, hunger or nibbling rats and wake refreshed and unable to stand, as the toes nibbled away. Be happy the prophesy fulfilled, "The Lord Our God feeds the sparrows and grows the lilies in the field," so who cares about rough sleepers, not the government so, why should ravenously ratites.

The ten meowing cats righted themselves and landed on ten heads doing terrible damage. Poor cats were frightened, disorientated after their fall.

The six rose pots sent six strollers after a heavy Italian meal to the emergency. Junior doctors with apartment bills helped them so took double the time to stitch and pull to get the electricity paid, and the Mercedes outside.

The twenty weed pots littered weed everywhere so police officers on horses found their steeds high and kicking people wanting entertained. The fallen police officers trained to shot anything moving, fired six rounds that makes thirty-six bullets at the horses, and missed, where did the bullets go, no one knows but rough sleepers sleeping on park benches found full of holes. Be happy for them, they got to spend weeks in a warm hospital bed, fed and able to ogle at male and female nurses.

The romantic couple because of the mayhem, lay nude on the

pavement embarrassed as mobile phones snapped their photos, soon uploaded, and hit a million times. Be happy, this is America, porn barons saw and hired them, and they became rich, buying tents on Miami beach, a rowing boat anchored in a marina, and a two-seater electric push bike.

Was this Roger's fault, he had thrown Peter out the window?

Or was it Peter's fault as his body crashed into innocent objects sending them cascading to the pavement a hundred feet below?

*

Three men approached Lizzy's apartment lemon yellow door. Lizzy liked to advertise a canary lived here, she is being the bird and suitors please leave gifts on the door mat.

The man who was in the lift was tall, dark, and handsome just as the tea leaves said he would be. Under an arm he carried a wrapped box in fancy paper covered in songbirds, a happy scene to put the recipient of the gift mentally in a happy expectant state, which would keep the smile of delight frozen as the gift turned out to be loathsome.

The second other man was olive skinned and waiting for the lift, he was tall, dark, and handsome too, so much so a Greek demi-god. He had tidied himself up after his quick decent from his cheap hotel window, yes it was Peter.

The third man was skinny and untidy, still in his jungle green adventurers' clothes, Australian Bush Hat with dangling fly corks, yes it was Igor, sorry, Steven; climbing the stairwell to reach Lizzy's floor sixteen fights up.

Steve kept it a secret he was asthmatic, well, Lizzy might not love him if see saw him coughing up mosquitoes in the jungle. On the long, lonely way up that stairwell no one heard him wheeze or gasp for breath as he continually muttered, "Peter, I am coming cough."

Peter had thought it a clever idea he takes the stairs just in case spotted and alarmed the prey, reality it was Peter's cruel nature surfacing. He did not want confined in a small lift with a man who needed to shower more frequently. There were also chitin remains about Steve's mouth.

You would not recognize Steven anymore the more. Steve listened to imps on his shoulder, dragging him into a dark pool of consciousness; here to do Roger De Jong's bidding. He was chewing, making crunching sounds, it was a cricket, he kept a packet of dried insects as a vitamin supplement.

To which man did Lizzy open the door to first? She was showered and perfumed in a light flower printed skirt.

"Fax," well it must be the tall, dark, handsome stranger but he was not a stranger. Amour lit up in her eyes, "Fax," she repeated softly, it was an invitation.

"Invite me in?" Fax said after a pregnant pause. He too glowed as realized not told, "bugger off." We can forgive Fax, he was slow when it came to women and most did tell him, "Bugger off." *It was the job see, not saying yet, read on.*

Lizzy stood aside letting Fax enter just as the lift doors shut to descend sixteen levels below, where Peter waited impatiently for the lift.

At level ten stairwell, Steve collapsed out of breath, no muscles, too much condensed milk, so he slid back to level nine, and found himself dangling staring down an empty draft filled stairwell.

He preferred not to look down, that petrified him so that he messed himself as his body weight became heavier and his knuckles whiter.

He was sure a bat was staring at him, "Are you rabid?" Igor, sorry, Steve as he feared that disease had spread to America by bats biting racoons, so Peter told him as he flicked cigar ash on him.

*

Calame and self, orbed down New York streets, packed with humans, bonny horses with no police on them, noise, bustle, so were not hurrying to Lizzy's, this was another Sandakan, just more buses, same street vendors selling food in buns not on noodles or sticky rice.

Then I felt blocked out of Lizzy, which alarmed me, so pulled Calame away from a monkey holding a tin cup.

"Something wrong with Lizzy," I warned Calame.

It was true as I found out soon enough. Lizzy had thrown out any thoughts related to me as Fax sat on a hard chair at a wooden table. A red wine glass half drank beside him.

"You left me, "c*** you," Lizzy spat at him softly.

"You went away to the East Indies, you left me Lizzy," Fax replied not a trace of anger showing, he knew he had one chance to amend things, so was staying sweet and cuddly, like Mr. Bean's teddy bear that gains the audiences sympathy.

"It was part of my vet job to investigate; besides, you were sniffing the pleats of that blond?" Lizzy accusingly.

"Never bedded her Lizzy, only have you in my mind as why I am here, just thinking about you," Fax only telling a half-truth as the blond-haired person rejected him because she knew he fancied Lizzy. Now Fax was back, showered, fresh underwear, his credit cards ready to spend.

"I like the gift, a battery-operated monkey beating a drum," Lizzy about to throw it at him.

"Yeh well in the battery compartment there isn't any batteries, have a look," Fax.

An opal pendant dropped out, one thing about Fax, he fished big, marlin, barracuda, shark, beautiful women, Lizzy.

"I can take this, thanks," Lizzy who realized if men wanted her, gifts helped, why not, she could remember them by the diamond ankle clasp, the gold bracelet, the opal clasp holding a bra closed, the wooden dinner table and six accompanying chairs. Lizzy did not have a high opinion of men apart from their usefulness in bed.

So, during the boring small talk Peter stood outside Lizzy's front door wondering where his Steve was?

"Master, help me?" Peter swore he heard repeated so followed the faint call and shook his head in disbelief, for an instant rage tempted him to stand on Steve's fingers and send him bouncing off the levels to the basement below.

Then Peter calmed down and taking off his jacket helped from below to grab Steven's legs and pull him into the stairwell. Something made of chitin ran down the legs and onto Peter who for an instant let go of Steve.

"Master save me," as Steve began to fall.

Peter grabbed the legs again as he looked for that insect, where did it go?

"Master," Steven on his knees kissing Peter's legs, who allowed the hero worship, which ended when he dragged Steve to Lizzy's door.

"I ring and you rush in, understand," Peter and gave Steve handcuffs. He watched fascinated as a dried worm went into Steve's mouth like a spaghetti strand.

"I think there is someone at my door?" Lizzy going to look through the spy hole, and seeing Peter and Steve unblocked me, so fear filled me and Calame.

Fax sensing trouble showed his 'FINEST BADGE' and small pocket revolver. Yes, he was one of them, THE FINEST out to protect you.

Peter never bothered ringing the doorbell, he burgled the keyhole and pushed the door open.

Steve rang in waving the handcuffs.

That made Fax hesitate shotting him as police carried handcuffs, burglars carried serrated knifes and loot bags.

Then Peter rushed in followed by Roger De Jong, so the room darkened. The insect on Peter bit him so he collapsed knocking his head on a spilled wine bottle rolling on the floor.

The darkness saved people going to emergency with bullet holes as Fax fired away, missing the lot, but not the neighbor's door opposite, and so alarmed was the resident, phoned the police for help.

Now Roger filled the room with friends, so Fax and Lizzy clouded mentally, well, it was the handcuffs on Lizzy and Fax's own on himself that allowed Peter to escort the prisoners to the lift. He was threatening them with Steve's serrated knife burglars carried as he rubbed the lump on his forehead.

Steve worried Peter more than the captives as he played with Fax's shooter. Lizzy looked at him in disgust, if this was the same Steven, he had allowed himself to become subhuman. Unfortunately, Steve understood her look and shot her.

Peter went berserk and took the gun and threw it into the stairwell, then kicked and tussled Steve in there so he bounced moaning crying, "Why master why, I love you."

Thankfully, there were two lifts, a small service lift that they crammed into as the main lift packed with armed police.

Thankfully, Peter saw that idiot Steve had missed Lizzy with his gunshot, but what had he shot?

Thankfully, Fax was happy the bullet was a small bore, 22, and had gone through his left ear lobe and not an eye or his forehead.

Peter noticed a sparkle amongst the blood on the ear, a gem set in an ear lobe after an ear piercing.

Fax was of the finest New York men, a police officer, tough, used to brawling with bad guys, finding grit in his burgers bought from street vendors, he got hungry on stakeouts, he had imagined he could take a bullet, but not the pain of having the remains of an ear ripped off.

He screamed loudly so even the police in the approaching lift heard. Their guns now unlocked as sure someone foully done to death.

Lizzy smiled, Fax was human, she was on the lookout for a crack in his hard man attitude, and now it had been given her, pain.

You could see it in Fax's eyes, glazed, his teeth were closed, he was tense and easily pushed in the direction Peter wanted him to go.

In the carport a laundry van was picking up used roller towels.

Sixteen levels up the lift door opened, and Steve fired into it from the open exit door. His bullets bounced about the lift forcing occupants down, firing as they flattened, bullet holes joined with the old in the neighbor's door that disintegrated.

Maniacal laughter drifted down the stairwell as Steve bounded down kangaroo fashion.

How he did these impossible anatomical leaps is mind boggling, spirits must have pitied him, adopted him as a pet, and carried him to the basement just like that 'Flying Monk,' so as the laundry van was driving off, Steve appeared across the windscreen, well, the back door was closed for Lizzy and Fax were behind the doors.

Peter only hit the brakes from shock, Steve was lying across his wind screen, "Get in here fool," Peter shouted at Steve.

Could have shouted,

"You are sacked, find someone else to screw up."

"You ugly pig, get off my windscreen."

"Where's that shooter, got to shot him."

"Close your eyes and he will be gone."

"Stop banging your head on the wheel."

So, Steve had time to join his master.

"Drive master, drive, the police are behind me," Steve and his foul breath swooned Peter. Steve ate lots of insects so, explains the breath essence and no garlic added.

To the basement they went to shelter amongst vampires, no, just kidding, they went down here as they had no were else to go. It was the negativity seeping from the carport that took Roger, ordering Peter to follow with the captives.

Extras appeared with high insurance for this scene, an old woman in a Zimmer who never made it out of the van's way, boy, she bounced all the way down the van roof and out of the story.

A skate boarder working as a drug mule next and as the van sped away, a skateboard twirled on the road, but no sign of the mule, he was holding onto a windscreen wiper of the van.

"Master look a spy," Steve referring to the skater and Peter switched on the windscreen wiper and the boy vanished under parked cars.

A small Jack Russell annoyed it jumped in the window and bit the blazes out of both, then ran away to a local butcher who gave her sausages.

"Master I am bleeding," Steve and Peter hoped a 'bleed out' was in process,

*

Calamity was holding onto me not allowing me to zero in on Lizzy.

"Ook," we are both grown women, "Ook," "I have sad news Henry."

"Is Lizzy dead," I joyed looking about the dimensions of Ether about us two.

"Ook," "Fax," the reply, "Fax," what was that a new Jockstrap for football players?

"Ook," and Calamity showed a mental picture of a police officer spotlessly clean, the brass badge gleaming, his teeth too, the hair showing so much gel, flying bugs got trapped there.

The back read, "To Lizzy my love, Fax, xxx."

I understood and died, but that was impossible, ok I became an anchor.

Calamity edged closer with a comforting arm over my shoulder. "Ook," "Cheer up, I am still here."

I started remembering our 'FLING' as that was what it was. How could I be so foolish to think a permanent relationship would evolve from our friendship? I should joy that I had met her and held hands.

"Ook," "friends like us," and Calamity wrestled me into a smooching position.

Half an hour later "Ook"," you don't love me," "as a friend, you ape, me human ghost, understand, yes?" Rotten fruit came my way as an answer.

Figure 9 1905 photo Roger DeJong

"You do not have a driving license, do you?" Peter asked Steve as he drove the laundry vehicle, and why this type of van, because movies in America always use them for these type of action scenes.

Then Peter added with his face pressed against a door to the van's compartment. "I was driving a moment ago, how did you get behind the wheel?" Well, it was his fault as he did not trust his Steve to check on the prisoners, so they swapped seats.

Peter was paying for it now as his jaw went sideways and his molars ground tongue. A diamond tongue stud lacerated his teeth, all would need capped; your cash made Peter rich. See, Peter had served a six month internship, forced upon him by the local unemployment office, to work with tax collectors when twelve, and he galvanized towards the shady, them that dangled a Dayak over an outboard motor for pennis earned selling shrunken heads, and when taken or not, the Dayak dropped in amongst the circling fins, as a lesson to others, 'GIVE ME give, give , me' but do not worry they have a wonderful Life Guard Service, a lifeguard who swam out and saved the Dayak so be happy.

Yes, be happy as the Dayak and lifeguard now participate in Prince Harry's wheelchair Olympics, a note from the storyteller here, "they were not our extras, we look after ours, just see our track record in the story."

Interlude over, never mind Steve was good at driving lesson number one, he had knocked off sixteen parked car taillights, run over a man obsessed with a mobile phone conversation, so never heard the wheels behind him, or smelt them burning rubber on him, just an extra hired for a free meal.

Steve went bumpy bump over ten rough sleeping folk whose legs stuck out from parked cars.

Terrified a cat into becoming a mummy cat in the back seat of an unknown car.

Two Doberman dogs unable to escape the parked vehicle they were in to get at Steve, took their frustration out on the car fake leather seats, leopard spotted P.V.C.

A small tidy lady using a Zimmer while her servant walked ahead with a bird cage, housing a thousand-dollar rare sparrow, into the path of the zigzagging laundry van.

"I like to eat birds as a pudding after an insect main," an idiotic servant of Peter.

A cage embedded with gems as the tidy lady was loaded, but that did not stop it being squashed.

Do not panic, the thousand-dollar rare sparrow flew away to breed with common household sparrows and lived happily ever after with thirty-six grandchildren.

Better not look at the servant that the laundry van tires left creases on, and the little old lady sat and had tea with the other old lady and her squashed Zimmer, they were identical twins.

Way behind the sixteen police officers tried to all cram into a commandeered vehicle, a Fiat Bambino. Luckily, it had a slide back summer roof as New York officers can be tall, or small and dumpy.

Four jumped the lift back up to ground where outside their

own spacious vehicles parked.

The rest ran after the swaying laundry vehicle pumping bullets into it and everything else in the dingy environment causing a million dollars of damage to parked cars, fire hydrants and shot up extras who claimed actor insurance, what insurance? "What they do not like employment conditions, they can go work as Lifeguards in Borneo, I hear there are vacancies," a storyteller.

Just as well mummy cat is heading for a new home in an animal rescue shelter, where she and her eleven kittens will be warm and fed in clean air.

In the back of the pursued van Fax had landed between Lizzy's legs.

Did Lizzy mind, I mean she had a ghost boyfriend, no Henry was a friend, an experimental entity you put on a Xmas tree for extra fairy lights, her excuse.

Fax was her hulk of a man from the past and reason she fled to Borneo with a broken heart. Henry was an old band aid found in the bottom of a drawer. Her drawers were emptied and wiped regularly, so it was not a dusty crumb infested band aid so germ and weevil free; somehow weevils are found everywhere.

But what she minded was Fax not making endearing delicious sounds but rather "I been shot, I am bleeding out, the maggot stole my diamond, what fly is driving this van?"

Lizzy felt her pants quickly wet, then get sticky as Fax's small amount of bleeding stopped and congealed. Fax had never bled before so really thought he was bleeding out.

Lizzy felt unclean.

Lizzy changed her knickers daily.

To shower daily.

Lizzy brushed teeth often, so teeth sparkled, as gem gifts used as teeth fillings, no mugger did ever think of pulling teeth, except one, Peter, "See you had to have gems as fillings to know where to look."

See, Lizzy sat on men clothed to encourage gifts from them, with words such as, "Diamonds are a girl's best friend."

Lizzy saw the pendant as future evidence against the fly at the wheel and send him away to a secure unit needing an insect repellent.

Lizzy let Fax break her heart, Lizzy slit her eyes, she needed more gifts to forgive, he cheated on her, she had to get checked for S.T.D. and never been so embarrassed in her life, "Sit here and open wide, I need a swab," yes lots of gifts to *never* forgive but keep taking till Fax was broke, then kick him out. The blood bleeding out from him might have A.I.D.S., now she panicked.

Lizzy needed to shift Fax's dead weight head from between her legs, cramp was setting in.

Lizzy tried pleading but Fax too immersed in self-pity, as well as "I will stay here as halfway home," manly type of thoughts.

Lizzy as 'all womankind had been taught by The Easter Bunny to wind silently.'

That moved Fax so he spent the rest of the journey rolling about the back of the van as now had no support.

Peter managing to look through the center window into the back compartment was amazed, spell bound, wondering what Fax did do next.

Fax's feet had opened with kicks ten smelly laundry bags that out smelled Lizzy's dainty windy that smelled of oranges and lemons.

His feet entangled soiled 'Y Fronts' as Fax grappled to stand enveloping him in waste stinks.

One he sent airmail to land on Lizzy's face.

Another hit the glass Peter was gazing out.

A Giant African Rat used for mine clearing ran out of black bag eleven and bit Fax someplace important, so he collapsed.

The rat ran between Lizzy's open legs, feeling safe and welcome, it was the scent of oranges and lemons, even limes that did it.

Lizzy dared not move a muscle.

Bag thirteen opened itself as has been justled too much and there was a man, his mouth taped, hands and feet tied, but he was blue, yes, a dark purple more like it, as a stocking wrapped his throat tight, it was a murder.

"Evening all," Roger making a grand entrance through the back of the van.

"What a stink, Lizzy?" Roger mistakenly identifying from whom the essence originated as he had a low opinion of woman.

Then the murdered body flushed through Roger's dark mist, followed by stinky washing, moldy pizza slices, a crucifix, "Hiss," Roger's reply wondering what idiot was driving the van.

Then he focused on Lizzy, their eyes met, the gaze held, it was so romantic but a lie, romantic for Roger only. He listened to harp music played badly by demonic imps who whispered, "She loves you."

"Henry helps me," Lizzy managed remembering she had blocked me and Calame out for her romantic evening with Fax, but then I did not know the reason then.

"Ook," Calamity shaking my ectoplasm excitedly, we were going to see Lizzy, shaken so violently, till I was no longer ectoplasm but white mist with mushy peas as MIND.

"Ook," Calamity embarrassed and not knowing where to look, as my ectoplasm melted in her hands.

*

Lizzy was calm as police bullets made ventilation holes in the van.

Roger giggled; their fast kinetic energy tickled.

Roger was in love, a first, "She will marry you, we will attend as guests," and that sobered Roger his dark entities lied.

Peter widened his eyes as bullets pinged, zinged, and thudded about his pressed face against the viewing glass for the back of the van. "Jesus please," but did not specify to Jesus what so Jesus left.

"An American roach heard so much about you," as Steve reached for the insect. "Look Master, no fingers on the wheel," which enabled him to fall amongst the driving pedals and eat the roach.

An animal loathed by millions of Americans as a pest.

"Lovely," Steve loving them instead, thinking of starting roach farms, and letting the insects loose so, he could have a fresh supply of wild protein, vitamin E, and sewage germs.

At last Peter pulled his sweat glued face off the glass and made interesting hand movements towards the wheel, was he making the sign of the crucifix, no, must be two finger signs, no it is a throttling move aimed at Steve.

"Oh, master no need to worry, Steve is here," and pushed Peter away. Sadly, just as a bullet punctured a back tire resulting in the van skedaddling to the left.

"To the zoo, oh goody, just where I wanted to go," Steve.

Peter slid headfirst unconscious onto the metal smelly floor, where a thousand soles had stood.

Thingy is, what had those thousand soles stood in before?

"Who is this moron?" Roger asked watching as spirits can through the Ether. Then looking at Peter his grandson snoozing on the van floor, his murderous intentions towards Steve turned to admiration, and Steve continued laughing as bullet energy passed through Roger shattering the wind screen.

Still Steve passed the wheel from hand-to-hand thinking

that is steering for you, so the van headed for the zoo gates.

'NEW YORK ZOO, HOME TO ALEX,' the sign said in the street-lights.

In the back Fax had vanished under a pile of dirty washing, a soiled diaper had slid into his mouth muffling his protests at the way life was treating one of New York's Finest. He should be rejoicing as those dirty whatever it took bullets with his name on them.

Lizzy was calm, a real wonder woman in red tights and silver bodice as she had planned a romantic liaison with Fax, till Peter and Steve's arrival. "Hey what about Henry?" "Who's that?"

I glared at her letting Calamity shield her with spirit energy. "Two timer," I thought, "Not at all, a girl needs to stretch her bodice, to be gifted gems to buy a condiment looking over Bondi Beach, a motorized surfboard to escape sharks, a queue of bronze muscular lifeguards at her door with gifts found on the beach, a wallet stuffed full of cash, a diamond studded watch, the papers to another condiment next door where a murder took place, what do you have against that Henry?"

She was right, a girl would be a wrinkled prune in two decades so had to make the best of where she sat, so accepted I was a moldy ghost.

So, Roger was admiring Steve's driving so much he wanted a try at the wheel so why he ignored us.

"Ah my headache," Peter trying to upend to look out a shattered windscreen. "God no," he screamed as he did not want to join Roger as a spirit.

"What is he shouting for?" I asked looking away from Lizzy. "Hold on," I added so Roger heard me. Never mind he was at the wheel or fighting for control of it.

"Master, remember me," Steve as Roger understood what doorhandles were made for, as Steve used one.

Steve sailed out just as the van collided with the impressive iron gates.

Yes, the gates bust open, yes, the van burst too and the remains went into the zoo making horrid sounds smoking also.

The van and gate collision were the reason the following police never saw Steve's undignified departure as he tried to steer his body away from a palm tree swaying in a gentle warm breeze. Songbirds sang 'Goodnight human, sandman coming to put sand in your eyes.'

"Carry them into the snake house," Roger commanded Peter who after one look at the captives negatively shook his head. He reached for a gun, but he did not have one, the idea to lessen the weight to carry; but he did feel Roger slap his head.

"Pick them up I said," Roger not like argued with, especially by aspiring relations to his crime empire. What crime empire, he has been dead a long time, a hundred years plus.

It was now me and Calamity floated out amid a hail of bullets aimed at palm tree branches as they looked shadowy humanoid, placards of ferrous beasts, a peanut vendor whose spilled nuts did be a welcome breakfast for local squirrels and a curious security guard who returned fire. His name was Jamie Ortez and had seen all the Die-hard movies. He knew he had to save the Zoo; exotic animal traders had arrived; Jamie would be a hero and citizenship.

Those in the van people fleeing the traders, zoo employers or why come here?

The police returned at least a hundred bullets to his six fired.

Jamie Ortez needed a strong weed, but that was against the law, so he just stood trembling, yes next to a humanoid palm tree branch, which absorbed his trembles so attracted another hundred bullets.

When it was over, Jamie was wide eyed, lower jaw stuck out, tongue out at an angle, dribbling spit that hit the grass he was on, spatting a deadly forked thingmabob that bit his exposed left hairy leg, see he was in shorts showing of his gym muscles and was zoo uniform copying a famous Australian snake handler, and he had horrid bendy hairy legs and knobby knees.

His muscles went into an apoplectic shock, so he collapsed to, 'We got him,' 'between the eyes,' 'no, I got him between the legs,' 'a free sex reassignment surgery,' laughter from the police side; they imagined an exotic drug dealer was ahead, they had watched all the 'Arnie' movies.

They could be throwing vipers and cane toads at each other, I was a ghost, could see and walk through the bullets.

"Ok," Calamity laughing as kinetic energy tickled.

I laughed like a hyena, loud, eerie, were-wolf sounding so combatants stopped.

A good thing for Jamie Ortez as the police stopped firing, it gave him time to look at what bit him, a scorpion, but was it just an ordinary scorpion or the deadly variety that you died under five minutes.

Out came his imitation Rolex, it needed five minutes shaking to make the hands move.

"Hey, I been here staring at this watch five minutes and still alive," Jamie and so happy threw the rubbishy watch away. It landed in the chimp enclosure, "Ook," meaning" Cool, a Rolex", a chimp now wearing it.

There was another almost forgotten soul in a palm tree that look shadowy humanoid, it would take five minutes for Steve to recover from bullets zinging about him, the dirty man from terror had 'done a dump,' 'Stinky Steve', we can call him, but wait a moment, he was already called that.

Anyway, shaking off the kinetic energy I followed a cursing, hunched over Peter, into the 'Reptile House.' "Wait till I get Steven?" He was saying, "This manual work is for him, not me," "Steven is paid to carry heavy captives," "What is this, a soiled Y

Front, I am going to vomit," and did, that did not impress Roger.

Smelly Y fronts smelt like pooh, reminding Roger of home, the lower energy levels of the crypt of heaven.

"Lizzy, we are here," I shouted into the Ether, so my voice was heard.

Lizzy looked towards me, there was Calamity's ectoplasm silhouetted in the reptile house doorway.

"Ook," Calamity copying me, so the police heard and saw her.

"A gorilla has escaped."

"Where did it go?"

"Loose," a police sergeant fresh from the movie 'The Last Legion,' and three hundred bullets headed towards Calamity but smashed every window in the neighborhood., scaring dumps out of folks watching the zoo, as television had a president in a blond wig on selling golf clubs, and was boring.

As Calamity had run through Roger and picked up the first human bundle she came across, and out through a window.

There was the groan of a human passing through a part open window, and the sound of breaking glass.

Bullets thudded where the window used to be. "Jamie are you safe, your pal Oli is here to save you," as the friend returned fire below the window.

" Jesus save me, and I will become a nun," a voice from the sack Calamity carried.

"There, an escaped ape got a hostage."

"Shoot it quick."

"Which one?"

"Jamie is that you in the sack, here gorilla we got lots of bananas, come to Oli."

"A gorilla got me, shoot it dead," from the sack so whoever

was inside had lied to Jesus promising to become a nun if saved, should be 'priest.' Then a frantic male voice added outside the sack, "Do not shoot, I am zoo security, do not shoot," as realized he did be full of a hundred bullets soon.

Anyway, "Wherever I go, you Henry turn up, you love me or something?" Roger and laughed at his joke.

Lizzy looked at me, wondering if Roger was right, wherever he was I was.

"No way Lizzy," and thudded into Roger as an angry white orb.

Growls heard as Roger's friends jumped onto me to protect him.

So many and the smell of unwashed Y Fronts held me down, so Roger escaped prancing over to Lizzy like a Napoleonic dandy with an extra-large sized cod piece.

Lizzy could not help herself but look and was impressed.

Peter spoiled everything as he ran and picked Lizzy up, throwing her over a shoulder. "What do American women eat?" He complained.

Roger also complained as he could stand in front of a mirror admiring himself, and now the mirror a woman he could flaunt in front of was in a 'poof' gone, by that idiot Peter.

Then the light coming through the busted reptile house window vanished, "Master it is me," and Steve was stuck, well he drank too much condensed tea.

Roger smiled; you could see that in his misted face in his dark orb. Here was a human, Steven that could teach Peter how to be villain and a man.

Below bullets had hit the lock of the anaconda widow, disintegrating it.

It was silent, one could hear the flicker of snakes' tongues.

KEITH HULSE

Peter hated snakes, they bit his men's, tourists, explorers, people who had Paid him to take them into the jungle ankles, then they died.

Because they were dead, the police tried to pin their murders on him; it was those hissing slithery thingmabob's at his feet now. That gave Peter superhuman strength and he was at Steven's head, pushing it out.

"Master, thank you, I love you," Steven said as he fell to the ground.

"Catch," Peter throwing Lizzy down to him.

Roger giggles away admiring Steve's intuition to flee with Lizzy. To stand and fight was to lose. Roger giggling, well more like a crocodile clearing a throat after swallowing a dozen cane toads. This Roger fascination of Steve was because Steve had all the criminal agility, he had hoped Peter had, and did not, that allowed me to tip toe past. Even his black misty friends tried to point at me but knew better than to disturb THE MASTER.

Peter edged away out of the Reptile House Front door, pressed against the wall, and followed the smell of sweetened condensed milk to Steve playing with the merchandise; outside the 'Cat House,' at Steve's feet part of the sign, shot away by a hundred police bullets.

'BIG,' it read.

Peter felt the flicker of a tongue on his right wrist so froze.

Calamity above on a slender bending cherry tree branch opening her sack.

Jamie Ortez led away by Oli to safety, at the back of the 'BIG CAT HOUSE.'

Roger was waving his dark mist friends to adore and worship him, just no hope for the few that were The Bad, Good and Ugly.

The owners of the hundred police bullets fired times ten rushed through the broken zoo gate and stopped.

There were big slithery snakes on the road in front minding their own business, the police did like to keep it that way.

Just serpents went this way and that, attracted by the smell of unwashed Y Fronts; why to a snaky person that was the smell of delicious rat, and was way past feeding time.

Others saw FREEDOM where a gate once stood, now filled with frozen police officers as, "No one move, it collaborates with sharks," a detective flashing his badge in the moon light at the snakes.

Figure 10 Everlasting smile of Calamity the orangutan. An auto spirit drawing by Henry through a local medium in 1906 Sandakan, and apported to Lizzy by Henry 2021.

Peter, remember, outside the Big Cat House felt the flicker of a tongue on his right wrist so froze. "My that is a big tongue, must belong to a big snake, better keep still," he advised himself and looked down and squeaked, a giant constrictor was sniffing Y Fronts, his.

"Ouch," Steve because Lizzy was free because an idiot called Steve, in his salivating efforts to reach Lizzy under ropes unwrapping her like a present, managed to have her knee him good. "Master I am done," he moaned staggering to Peter.

"Let me help you," Lizzy and pushed so Igor, sorry, Steven fell upon Peter, treading upon the giant snake.

"Eek," Steven and froze in terror while Peter said, "You are sacked, go away, go home," as coils wrapped about Peter.

"Master you are my home," and Steve broken-hearted went into the Cat House leaving Peter to fate.

"I am hiding," Lizzy seeing Roger and his dark friends coming so went into the Cat House, "Lizzy, I am here," me, Henry to soothe and comfort her in my ghostly arms, stroke her red hair and whisper sweet nothings.

"Where the hell have you been, late, I been in hell and back, lazy ghost?" Lizzy demanded.

Meanwhile as Lizzy was becoming fed up with men, physical and ghostly, as only wanted one thing, 'DOMINOES with mushrooms,' "We will hide in here, better than staying still, these snakes climb up you as are mistaking you for a tree," Oli leading a zombified Jamie in with a dozen deadly tree vipers at home on him.

"Hiss," the snakes hissed.

"Hiss," from poor Jamie's bladder.

"Ook," Calamity throwing Fax in as she was in the huffs, see Fax had not returned her kisses, instead spent minutes digging ectoplasm out of his mouth. He knew he had rabies now, well Steve might, remember Borneo and a monkey that bit him in the Sandakan Seafront Hotel? See, the black bag Calamity took had Fax in it not Lizzy, silly monkey, or was it intentional?

"Peter, what are you doing?" Roger demanded seeing Peter wrestling with the boa constrictor. "Be like Steven, drop the snake and help him with Lizzy," Roger seeing Steve disappearing into the Cat House, where Lizzy went.

"Help me please, I am being swallowed," Peter begged his ancestor.

"Stop exaggerating Peter," Roger and followed Steven.

"Oh, Sweet Mother of Jesus save me," Peter half in the big snake's mouth and did feel his shoes dissolve in the snake's digestive juices.

"Do not tell Roger," Voices in Peter's head as dark mists possessed the snake.

"Cough," the snake went.

"Coughing," and Peter came out dripping snake whatever.

"Wait till I get Steven," he promised.

"Do not do that, Roger is going to adopt him as favorite son, Roger will do nasties to you," the dark voices in Peter's head. All Peter could do was gingerly step over fleeing slithers getting away from the advancing human police officers.

Now the dark spirits had left the constrictor it now rose twenty feet swaying in the moon light about to swallow Peter in one go.

"Mummy," Peter mumbled but did not pee himself as his bladder was empty, its contents being in the snake's tummy helping to keep the snake warm and cozy.

Then a hundred bullets zinged by the snake, not one bullet harming it but hitting a humanoid palm branch nearby.

"Snooze," the giant snake falling asleep on top of Peter as a vet had fired a sleep dart into it.

"Get up lazy and help Steven," Peter heard Roger, so did the bullet owners as spirits can vocalize their voice into the Earth realm, so Peter ran cowering into the Cat House as two hundred bullets followed him not a hundred.

Smashing all the locks on the cages which annoyed occupants, big cats awoken rudely from dreams of chewing keepers, swallowing tourists, running free in a zoo free of humans as all eaten, and there were Lizzy, Fax, Peter, and Steve with these words in fluorescent lettering, "DINNER."

"Lizzy climb up," I instructed my ex showing her a fire ladder going to the roof. "Cur," watching her go up. Then an ape covered my eyes, "Ook," "No peeking."

Steve followed her gaze; big cats were not small chewable insects and Steve using Lizzy as a step bounded up reaching the ladder that came down with his weight.

"A real Tarzan," Roger impressed watching Steve grab Lizzy

by the hair and go up as the ladder retracted.

"Never pull a woman up twenty feet by her hair Steven," I thought to him and that alerted Roger to my presence.

"Kill him," he ordered his dark friends.

So, never saw Peter run and leap to get a hold on Lizzy's feet.

"No, please do not come off," he begged as Lizzy's unlaced trainers began to slip away.

Under him a hybrid Sabre toothed tiger waited for him. The cat was part of a secret breeding program to make a crowd puller, a cat with long incisors with a T bone impaled. To make you ravenous and use the zoo restaurant.

Calamity above on a slender bending cherry tree branch was opening her sack remember.

Jamie Ortez now led away by Oli to safety, at the back of the 'BIG CAT HOUSE remember.'

Who was Oli, Jamie's cousin and an extra needed to keep Jamie in the story?

I, Henry full of Lizzy disconcerting thoughts arrives having sneaked past Roger.

"Ook," Calamity which translated, "Oh, Henry forgive me, he was so handsome," and Calamity held up Fax, gave him a kiss goodbye and dropped him.

Well, he had sworn to protect the public and that is what he did, passed Peter now holding Lizzy's toe tails who was amazed they were slipping away in his hands, toenails hand painted with stars, moons, others painted hearts, he was amazed females had a spare set of toes.

"Meow," the saber-toothed cat opening wide a mouth to greet Fax.

"Mummy," Fax sprinting from that cat mouth at sixty miles per hour, away into the darkness and FREEDOM.

Just when I was about to descend onto Steve to save my ex-girlfriend, guess who grabs me.

"Henry, always Henry, curse you," Roger passing Calamity.

"Bye Mr. Henry," Roger hanging onto Lizzy's real toes as Steve ran off into the dark empty zoo streets dragging Lizzy by the hair Cur, would not like to be either when she gets FREEDOM.

An oliphant trumpets passing by winding as was nervous so green gas filled Roger who blinded went back towards the police and with his dark friends, trained to protect Master, unlike Steve who was out to kill his Master, of course unintentionally as lacked ambition.

"Ook," Calamity holding Henry tight, so I was A PRISONER of ectoplasm.

And the night filled with the laughter of dark entities as a thousand police SWAT bullets full of kinetic energy, went through them, destroying every building in the zoo, and the animals knew FREEDOM.

Of course, the fire sprinklers went off soaking the SWAT team, the ordinary police officer, the newly arrived fire fighters, the press, ogling pedestrians, but not a creature was wetted, dry and cozy as some unseen creative power kept them.

*

"Master where are we?" Steve being polite to his master Peter, even offering Peter a creepy crawly found, an act of kindness that drained the murderous intentions out of Peter.

"He is only a simply idiot, see I will throw a stick and he will fetch," and Peter threw a stick and simple Steven carrying Lizzy disappeared into the darkness. Steven did not return the stick.

"Where did that idiot go?" Peter asked peering into the darkness but heard a woman scream and an idiot scream for joy, Xmas had come early, then an idiot shout, "Master, I am done, save me."

So, Peter followed.

An oliphant followed him.

Fax sprinted by at sixty miles per hour.

Snakes slithered heading the same way as Peter, so he cried, "Mummy."

"Let us find Lizzy now Calamity," I urged having stretched my orb to escape an ape's clutches.

"Ook," Calamity offering me a banana. But to no avail, that oliphant gassed so much it interfered with the electromagnetic electricity of our spirits, in other words, lost souls.

"Ook," Calamity adding, "But we have FREEDOM."

So never saw Steve climb walls and yellow cab roof tops hopping from one to another.

"I do not know how he does it, but I am hiring a taxi," Peter but was thrown out by the taxi driver for he stunk of oliphant smells, and worse, had slithers coming out of his pocket, and it was with a mighty scream he zoomed after his servant, Steven who carried Lizzy.

Now Lizzy had freed fingers so spent her time picking a bald patch on top of Steven's head.

Oh, fresh Ether tastes so nice in FREEDOM, but THE GAME WAS ON again, and we gave chase and just had to follow an oliphants trumpeting.

An elephant that big just goes through walls, and did, and soon all types of beasts was running a mock in the zoo grounds.

Steve was heading for the museum, where horrid artifacts of torture were on display, to give Lizzy a choice, them, or him so gave a werewolf laugh, ever heard one, either have I so might sound like a hippopotamus laughing.

"Why is that idiot Peter leading the police to my museum?" Roger only seeing Peter following Steve.

*

"We are here," I said to Steve and Lizzy in the museum.

"What is that?" Steve looking at Calamity in her super ape masked cape defender outfit. See we had hitched a lift on the back of an oliphant so where here, and here also Steve, he had not a chance in the world against us, as Steve fainted from an oliphant gassing. The gas being so solid did not rise and poison us, we were spirits.

The museum door opened, and a stink blew in, there stood Peter who jumped Steve, "I hate you," but the gas shrouded him, and he fell asleep in Steve's arms sucking a thumb.

Well, that meant we just picked a sleeping Lizzy up and took a lift on an oliphants back, yes, the same one that took us here as had smashed through the museum door.

Later, Steve and Peter were nowhere seen, and we cheered immensely they had met their demise under an oliphants four feet.

"Hip hooray," I shouted.

"How cruel you are?" Lizzy comparing me to boyfriends. Heck, she can feed crocodiles with extras hired as villains and I cannot celebrate DEATH to them two smears back on the museum floor?

"Ook," Calamity agreeing with Lizzy, "Ook," meaning love had blinded her from seeing the real me.

"I am a ghost, the real me, a white orb so is a good chap not like Peter and Steve," I protested. That is when Fax caught up at sixty miles per hour and began to flutter, out of steam.

Recognizing him I watched him begin to go to the rear, "Oh please Mr. Oliphant please," I am hoping for gas.

"Henry, your cruel man," and as Lizzy and Calamity passed shoved me off the Oliphant.

How those two helped Fax onto a moving Oliphant is anyone's guess. I marveled then let jealousy consume me, just for an instant, a puff of red smoke left my orb, and I was nice guy again and joined them.

"Say hello to Fax," Lizzy aloud forgetting Fax could not see me, but was wrong, all see orbs.

Now Fax wondered if his **girlfriend** were having a mental breakdown from all this trauma, so he relaxed thinking his girl-friend would not cast up the past.

But strange sounds came from his stomach as he relaxed too much.

I smiled, how could Lizzy date a STINKER?"

"Because he is kind," she lied to me as she knew him as a two-timing bum, self-serving and egotistic. Where people swung a silver cross from their necks, his was a pendant with his smiling face in it. She suspected Fax of bowing to it and decking it out with rose petals.

All this had read in her mind as was a ghost.

"Cheating," Lizzy, so I asked, "why date him?"

"He is terrific in bed, he is a physical, he buys me presents," and Lizzy played with her new pendant with an opal in it.

"Ook," Calamity at me.

"But what about us?" I asked heart broken.

"A fling."

And Fax showed the pendant about his neck at me to scare me away, and it worked for I laughed so much I vanished.

"Ook," Calamity wrapping furry ectoplasm arms about Fax and smooching.

The pendant was stuck in her mouth with these words, "Demon begone," and Calamity so hurt sought me.

"We are alone baby, come here," Fax overestimating his good looks but Lizzy, "Never cheat on Lizzy," and Lizzy beat the stuffing out of the two-timing handsome toothless cauliflower faced bust lip black and blue police officer.

"S***, she really does love me," Fax just before he passed out.

*

"Hello," it was Peter having hung onto the oliphants tail and crawled his way up to us.

Never hold an oliphants tail when the oliphant is nervous and has the runs.

"Look it is me," Steve and Calamity desperately replied, "Ook," "I have a man," grabbing Fax and loving him who 'NIL DESPARATUM', never gave up freeing himself from the ape's clutches so won his FREEDOM.

Now Steve avoided runny banana as he had held onto other places below looking for crunchy ticks and giant fleas, for insects are big on an oliphant.

"Never pull a woman by her toenails," Lizzy and karate chopped Peter so he "I am sailing," away off the oliphant tour.

"Master, I will avenge you, Bo Ho," but Steve heard as he crunched away, "never pull a lady by her hair," and kicked Steve heaps all over so he tumbled off the oliphant tour.

Now Roger fed up worshipping himself, had caught up with Peter.

"You stink," were his only words to his ancestral offspring.

Never mind, Peter had lots of company as ten thousand dung beetles escaped from the Insect House, attracted by his perfumes, now covered him. Then Steve tumbled by, bumping into the pointed ends of tumble weed blowing about the Virginia meadows so shouted often, "ouch."

When an oliphant runs it runs so ran.

"Steve my adopted heir," Roger aghast at Steve colliding with giant cacti extras, are in all movies filmed in America.

And Peter hurt inside, "Steve this and Steve that, Steve wonderful, Steve the good cook," and fed up with it. It was from this moment on he plotted to murder them both, and did it occur to his deranged manured mentality, Roger already was dead?

Well, he was about to get his chance as a bright light appeared over him.

"Oh, Jesus forgive my sins," and Peter fell on the baby rattlesnake and was bit on his nose, so it glowed red and swelled. "Now I will get my chance to murder Roger," as he saw demons come out of the light, but he was disappointed as the figures levitated him into a brilliant room, where he said, "Judas, needles, I am afraid of needles," and the figures pumped anti venom into Peter saving his worthless soul.

"Darn, I will have to cancel the party arranged for Peters arrival," Roger and drifted into the space craft.

As for the baby rattle snake, the aliens studied it. Just like we do to aliens in AREA 51, but with a difference, when they had finished zipping the snake back up, they let it go in the wilds to mate and breed and bite hill walkers and those celebrating the 5th of July at picnic sites.

Kind gentle aliens.

"Jesus must have forgiven me," Peter looking at alien girls.

"Master, I am with you always," Steve's grinding voice in Peter's ears and Peter knew Jesus was assessing him as to how he would react to Steve, he whom he planned to murder. (He was to wait till Steve fell asleep then disappear in the night, knowing Steve could not survive in the human world without him.)

Now below an oliphant saw the lights in the sky approaching and trumpeted, a sign of aggression and charged to nearest hated things it could see, two human cousins about to be eaten by big cats, so the Oliphant saved Jamie and Oli becoming dry bones.

Yes, say hello again to Jamie and Oli, cousins united, cousins about to die. Cousins who had hid in the back of The Big Cat House, and when the big cats escaped. "We are cat food," Oli rightly thinking, as Jamie was still suffering from a nervous breakdown said nothing.

It was the big cats themselves coming out at breakneck speed to escape slithers and the U.S. Army now arrived as Lights in the sky seen in the night sky above the zoo been reported, an alien invasion fleet was landing on the top of the demolished reptile house.

And the soldiers stood with the SWAT, ordinary police officers and fire fighters chatting to the locals who brought out deck chairs and barbecue ovens, a local shop owner opened to sell known beers, and because he was opened drug addicts ran into his shop to help themselves to tins of condensed milk.

"Help, I am being rob," and the 'FINEST' did not help as were waiting for the aliens to go away, their excuse, might be the slithers, lions, the laughing hyenas, and skunks gassing that put them oft moving.

"I am going to help myself for God helps those who do," the shop keeper and went back in the shop and found his Colt hand-gun and emptied it on the thieves, missing them all, but they dropped the tins of condensed milk and fled, Philippi Oli Jamie Santander was a hero and wondered where his cousins, Jamie and Oli were in the zoo, hoping them safe.

"I have prayed to every saint there is, so I know you are safe," he said sweeping up bullet ridden tins of condensed milk, but he was insured so was happy.

So, far the cats were knocking into the cousins, who fumbled onto a feline back, and stayed there as the mouth was up front.

"Cousin, how do we get off?" Jamie asked Oli who was always the savior of a situation.

Silence as Oli had not a clue apart from when they eat one of us, the other runs to safety, and where was safety, the woods out here were rumored infested with BIGFOOT. Oli just knew, even if Jamie was eaten, he did be eaten by BIGFOOT.

So, Oli said prayers to The Virgin Mary as he was from New York State.

"Oh Jesus," Oli seeing Mary in the lights above and not little green men, "Jamie we are saved," as an oliphant weighing a ton thundered into them, as a light from the light above shone on them, illuminating, making them easy targets for an angry oliphant.

Would Mary save the believers, or would they become squashed tomatoes?

*

Now Lizzy sat atop the oliphant she named 'Teddy Roosevelt,' in honor of that man. I am not sure if Teddy was pleased having a banana runs oliphant named after him, somehow, Lizzy was taking the micky.

So, I found out by touring Spirit thinking of the real Teddy.

"An elephant named after me, brilliant and charges up hills like me, feed it more bananas," he replied to me, so I had an excuse to return to Lizzy.

"Still intact," Lizzy peeking under elastic that she stretched wide, then let go.

"By all the saints I am bitten by slithers," Fax awakening to an elastic Y front sting.

"What is she like?" Lizzy asked meaning 'THE OTHER WOMAN?'

I eavesdropped, Lizzy was aware I was here and said nothing, Fax was afraid of ghosts and falling of the oliphant and then get bit by a scorpion or Gila Monster or married off to an ape.

"You are the best Lizzy, always will be, I love you Lizzy," Fax in defensive mood.

Lizzy evaluated his tripe, why do boys repeat themselves every scenario.

"So do I," I sneaked in giving Lizzy roses in her mind, then with pleading a ghostly Mormon Choir singing heavenly hymns, peaceful, making a woman's mind tranquil to me.

No smile, she knew what I wanted, a Ghost Romance or was it Fax she wanted squirming, no man cheated on her, it would take more pendants from Fax to share a dining table, with strong alcohol to finish the meal and after a year of gifts she would tell him to 'CLEAR OFF.'

Lizzy was no foul, no one pulled her hair, toe tails or cheated on her.

I smiled and sent in a Hawaiian beach scene with her lounging there, nearby a white orb and a ghostly arm appearing to rub sun oil onto her back, "I never cheated," I whispered.

An ape server in a large bikini approached with chilled soda drinks.

Lizzy smiled; I was winning.

Fax mistook the smile as forgiveness for him, he suddenly pulled her to him, smooching, slurping, breathing his last and ending my winning streak.

Fax now saved as a light appeared above us and the next, the physicals knew they were in a room with other physicals, wonder who they were?

"Aliens Calamity, ever been to Mars?" And with that drifted to that light.

"Ook," an ape throwing away a server outfit and putting on 'Super Ape,' the masked defender dress again.

And the space craft doors were about to shut when, "90756756," an alien to another alien who replied, "90567867806757063," and the next an oliphant and two cousins imported up.

"75367900390," the first alien slapping the head of the second alien, "that is an oliphant, want to crush the humans, eh? Eh? Stupid Igor, what are you, stupid?" Translated.

And stupid, the alien called Igor cried big sobs as it mentally led the oliphant to another room, we two had a peek, "Ook," Calamity wanting to stay with the oliphant, for the room was a savannah, with banana trees, and holographic oliphants to keep the real one happy.

"Ook," 'me too,' Calamity hoping for a male chimp or three in there. That ape just thought of nothing else but males, ape, chimp, human, pets, parrots if it was male and figs.

*

"Just like the zoo cousin," Oil sweeping up oliphant pooh.

"Ouch my back," as Igor the alien whipped the molasses out of him, so Oil had to sweep that up too.

"%$^&*(() &*(&*," the alien, 'my name is Igor, I am your Queen," Igor and because the aliens were smooth skinned everywhere, they had no need for pockets, their mind controlled mental pockets and Igor's pockets stuffed with dried insects?

"Look Jamie look, we have nothing like that back on earth," Oli watching Igor pull out of thin air, and the air was thin, a packet of insects and gobbled them all.

The invisible door opened summoned in the mind of the first alien, "4684767564989?" "NO WHIPPING THE ANIMALS, LOOK A SIGN, HAVE YOU READ IT?" He asked and took the whip away from Igor, and sent Igor and the sweeping crew to us, where we sat with crossed legs for the aliens did not need toilets, they got rid of their waste mentally, and explains sudden dog pooh on a pavement that was sparkling clean a moment ago, and you squelched it.

I sped over to Lizzy, "You ok," and deliberately excluded 'Baby you, ok?'

"Baby, you, ok?" It was Fax not forgetting where he had left off.

"& (&*&^%OO(7?" Igor the alien noticing Steve pull out a packet of sour cream locusts, "Want one, yummy," Steve rubbing his belly, now round and exposed, a hairy wobbly Mr. Blobby.

"That is not Jesus, maybe Lucifer, but not Jesus," Peter deeply knowledgeable in what Jesus looked like so could identify him.

And behind Igor who shared Steve's locusts an alien girl, "Now that is more like it," Peter and Fax who was about to take Lizzy in his arms who did kill him for that, was saved death from Lizzy by looking too.

"These aliens do not wear clothes Fax," Lizzy sternly, and was a warning, the sternness, so Fax heard and did not pick Lizzy up into his arms, he was ogling.

"Ouch," Fax as Lizzy poked his ogling eyes, "pervert," she explained.

"Will you marry me Igor?" Steve on one leg so slapped about by Peter as Steve was an easy target.

And Peter remembered his murderous intentions to Steve, so slapped him mercilessly laughing.

"It is cool with me master, slap and kick me and bite me all you want for I love you," Steve and everyone present was ill.

"%&^^$" £5667$£," 'That Steve is my boyfriend human," Igor for Igor was a girl and with her mind showed Peter a brush and oliphant as Jamie and Oli needed relieved.

"Ha, my Steve will take over this spaceship and I will captain her," Roger DeJong suffering illusions of grandeur.

"Lizzy, with your cowboy spirit and my clocking camouflage, we can take control of this ship and go home," then the handsomest alien general or whatever entered our room, and an alien girl ghost at that in a tight-fitting alien skin, as they did not wear cloths. Lizzy and that jealous ape watched me intently to see what I was watching.

Ch 11 Aliens Exist

"The ones standing in front of us captives were alien women, so we googled and uttered not a complaint, in the hope of a romantic attachment, we were all 'LONEY TUNERS.'

I was no longer staring at Lizzy but this alien ghost in front of me, even in death these aliens wore nothing.

Lizzy was no longer staring at me or Fax but at this Tarzan of an alien who to show off his physic, his triangular body tapered into a lion clothe. Little green men also printed on the lion clothe and the men were eating alien hot dogs. It was this alien idea showing he had a sense of humor, get the girls laughing so much they were on the way to Jupiter with him before they noticed.

Igor was blushing, Steve still knelt on sore knees needing to bend. The pain in his knees sent twitches to his eyes, in a moment he did fall left or right, let us bet as to which, and then he fell forward into Igor who looked about for the boss, no boss, and the smooching that went on between these two was horrid, every now and then the sound of an insect being crunched and a gulp of air.

Peter stared at them wide eyed and open mouthed. He was thinking suicide or double murder as he did not want to be in a world full of baby Stevens, they grew up. Let us feel happy for Peter for once, "Jesus have pity on me," now for a murderer he liked to speak to Jesus and The Lord did as alien females took Peter away.

"Take me to your leader," Peter joked as meant 'harem' and thanked Jesus, see speaking to The Lord again. Since he was in a mental paradise never noticed Roger fuming over his weakness for unblemished women with no clothes. Look these alien girls had everything under their tight skin, it was human imagination that did the rest, and ghostly.

"Close your eyes Peter, we have work to do, what work?" Roger realizing, he was no longer on Earth, what were his ghostly priorities? He had no idea, even forgotten Ramapithecus in all the exciting chases.

Then remembered, Kill Henry, but he was already dead. Kidnap Lizzy, done, and so felt empty. Then promote Steve to adopted son, but he was ignoring him thanks to an alien naked woman, 'no clothes again, what gives with these aliens?' Roger screamed, when Roger spoke you listened and not share the same insect, and Roger was sick and thankfully because he was in Spirit no mess, just as well as alien robotic cleaners watched him, swinging mops like clubs; they had no sympathy for Roger, and what is this? Artificial intelligence could see Spirit?

Apart from the robotic whir of electric motors, silence greeted Roger.

Oh, back to priorities, Roger has Peter marry Lizzy, so she willingly went with them, because Peter was handsome and Steve ugly as sin, then divorce her and hand her down as seconds to Steve and after time with him, she did be eating insects and calling Roger, "MASTER." But he was wrong, did be calling Steve Master and beg for more Satsuma flavored insect biscuits.

Where was Steve, gone with Igor to where, of course to see her insect collection, so Roger fumed.

"And that monkey, Calamity, she was dead too, is nothing going right for me, and why is that monkey wearing a masked defender outfit and ape mask? If that monkey can wear one, I can to", and Roger thought up a catalogue of stretchy outfits he could wear.

There was 'Masked Demon,' 'The Were-Ghost,' he liked that as he got to howl, 'Bat ghost,' and a little robin that held seven black belts popped up from nowhere was good too.

Roger so immersed never saw a ghost appear, an alien angel come for him to make Roger become a sparkling white orb.

And Fax "Hello baby, my name is Fax, like my biceps?" Fax to an alien he supposed was a beautiful girl.

"Hi handsome, my name is John," the alien replied mentally, squeezing Fax's biceps.

That leaves Oli and Jamie, men just relieved not to sweep up oliphant droppings, were happy to be led away to the same place as Peter. Second hand undocumented immigrants come cheaper than union extras, so foolishly gloated over the female attention. As cheap zoo staff, the only female attention they got was dish washing for the female restaurant dish washers. Did they hate women now, not at all, creamed mushroom, half bitten tortillas, a sausage roll, food to eat was found in the dish water, they loved the job.

So, the female chimps threw the teacups with scalding tea onto them to make them hate women?

The female Condor bird although on a chain, made them the soft lining for her twiggy nest to hate women.

The female wolves after a good chewing to give them as tender steaks to their pups to make them hate women.

The snakes bit them and needed closer examination to see if it was a male or female, in the meantime you were turning blue waiting for the anti-venom.

Yes, did Oli and Jamie hate all women after these horrendous work experiences?

And less we forget, our oliphant was a girl oliphant and covered them in what they were hired to hose away. And they loved Frederick the oliphant as someone, a vet needed glasses to see that Frederick did not have those important male's thing-amabobs, so was a girl.

"Maria Ortez Santander Chili Mexico Mayan Philipp de la Cruz Oliphant", and the oliphant was oblivious to such noble heritage, but she did love these two and did trample anyone who she saw hurt them, after a warning trumpet as elephants were sneaky fighters, as the trumpet call was followed up by a charge by a ton beast from behind a rose bush it had been hiding, watching you slap the back of the heads of these extras for not un-blocking zoo sewers, were flushed down pythons, crocodiles and baby animals had gone, now grown up as human haters, and Oli and Jamie were humans, the reason for the slap.

And after Maria the oliphant finished with you, you needed emergency.

"We are blessed, The Virgin Mary looks after us," Jamie leaning on his bucket full of stinky water.

"Yes, Mary has given us good jobs," Oli using a ten-foot brush that squirted soap and disinfectant to wash Maria the oliphant's teeth, no, for the smelly bum fool.

And the oliphant never felt the tranquilizer in the rump.

"£&^%&*&**((," the alien boss needing a hundred of her kind to levitate the one-ton oliphant to the LABORATORY.

"Hey, this is not a boudoir?" Peter seeing vials with shrunken heads in them, a ticket hung from one, Sandakan Market. Other glass tanks with slithers that bit the glass to get at him, and Peter recognized one, a bit of his expensive silk tartan trousers stuck to a fang. "Where have you taken me, I am Peter, the handsomest villain in Sandakan, look at my smooth hairless legs, shaved every day, my teeth so white you see the moon, and my eyes, the twinkle of the Boudoir, so, "darlings where have you brought me, ouch?" Peter as one of his beautiful abductors stuck a blunt needle in his bottom, always the bottom, and the rest giggled at his printed shorts, now stiff from his adventures, and they needed changed, and smelled of pee, and other stuff as he had been wearing them from day of boarding an airplane to get to America, The Land of The American dream, where the poor can become President without a revolution.

And lo, in a swimming pool, it was a huge LABORATORY, a swimming pool with crocodiles, and from their teeth, clothing and belts belonging to the extras Peter had hired way back on the river to Sandakan, and in the story disposed of. See, be happy, no bodily remains, just clothing which means the extras lived to tell the tale, who are to recommend this story as they get 0.0005 percent royalty per book sold of this tale.

That is generous, yes, since Jamie and Oli were charged for meals, loo rolls, electricity to iron their uniforms as did not have citizenship.

Now it was only Calamity hiding behind banana trees in the hologram room that saved our foolish hides, saved us from what, THE LABORATORY were machines would turn us all males into Steven clones and all girls into Igor clones.

That is more in line with Interplanetary Exploration than what they do to aliens in Area 51, THE HUMAN LABORATORY.

And as no member of the public had survived sneaking into

Area 51, we can only go by what people who worked there have said, "Alien autopsies, yes, little green and grey men with big black eyes, naked, with four long fingers, and speak with their minds, screaming at you, "I am still alive."

IS THIS WHY A LABORATORY EXISTED ON THIS CRAFT, telepathic communication between those in AREA 51 and the crew of this space craft? REVENGE was at work, with blunt needles and rusty scalpel, "%&^$£," "REVENGE," Igor's boss and laughed.

"$^% (*)," "get DNA samples," "&^$%%^," "so we can make hybrids," "^%$$££"", "and repopulate Earth with smiling Tarzans and Janes."

Igor looked at Steve who smiled, she showed no smile, but it was her eyes twinkling that led Steve out of the Laboratory back to the hieroglyphic room, where relaxing piano music played, a log fire burned, and dim lights and bowls of dried insects as treats.

"I can forget Master Peter for a while, tee he," Steve.

"Lizzy," the alien hulk in that printed piece of swimwear to Lizzy leading her to a corridor that led to a mile of corridors, and they managed the miles as sat on an electric caddy.

"Whir," the electric motor of the caddy.

Lizzy now overcome by the alien's lack of a hairy back and armpits, and so marvelous not having an overpowering smell of body odor mixed with perfume pongs.

The alien looked at Lizzy with big blank black eyes, they twinkled electricity into Lizzy who went into a nymphomaniac state, just as Igor had with Steve.

Elsewhere Peter admired his women alien guards, this was Jesus's reward to him for all the prayers he ever said, which were those mentioned above, and explains why he was thrown onto a cold hard high trolly, where straps held him still.

"Sadism, is it?" Peter had read his 'UFO' magazines drinking condensed milk tea, and unlike Steve afford a dentist who made sure his teeth were sparkly white and his breath garlic free.

"675554odfhhfdjhj7", "we read human minds and memories and see you are a stinker", "jfdjjfd7754"," we will mix your DNA with venomous creatures and your siblings will be where monster alien soldiers, to die for the glory of aliens everywhere."

So, stuck blunt needles into Peter and yes, a rusty scalpel used for an 'Ounce of skin.'

"Peter stop screaming, show them what you are made off," Roger drifting in to watch in the arms of an angel, but Peter showed them he was pepper, vinegar, and dried fish proteins. Peter looked at Roger, "Change places?" He asked Roger in a high-pitched scream as an alien roughed the specimen.

Roger looked the other way and hid his face in the heavenly smell of his angels' feathery wings. Roger now pacified by the harp music, all violent thoughts leaving him, "Are those boobs?" Roger asked the angel putting out an ectoplasm hand to find out. Just as he was about to touch Peter screamed as a kidney pulled out of his mouth.

"Disgusting Peter, you got two anyway," were Roger DeJong's famous words before the angel tussled him up and kicked him down to hell so Roger never found out if they were 'boobs?'

"I thought we had a flame going?" Roger engulfed in flames.

The angel burst out laughing and, Roger's dark entity friends cleared off. That was some angel, she had a mass of curly black hair under a diamond tiara and had stuffed her body into an UNESCO striped bodice, and her legs in knee knee-high boots.

"Baby, I love you," Roger called to this 'WONDER WOMAN ANGEL," and his friends stopped to see what happened next, bad mistake for this moving UNESCO bodice was upon them.

"Do not miss that little one hiding under you right sole," Roger being helpful, so do not be sorry for Roger, he had his friends with him roasting away their days.

I saw what happened to Roger, "I am the good guy, he was the bad guy," I said to my alien escort and zoomed away, passing Igor and Steve boarding a lifeboat and exiting for the dark side of the moon.

It was these two I owe my deliverance, as my escort left me to raise the alarm, and guess what, out in the corridors my mind cleared, "must be drugged air back in reception and laboratory," I concluded and remembered guilty Lizzy.

"She was finished with me, Fax and now this Mr. Universe alien 'Arnie' look alike. Yet it was only Lizzy I wanted, had I burned my bridges to her?

"Ook," Calamity apporting hundreds of burning candles to me, "Ook," "these are drugged Henry," and I began to swoon back into a drugged stupor.

Calamity left me in a lifeboat, obviously she intended to fill it with human physicals as I as a ghost did not need a lifeboat. Then seeing how dark and cozy the interior of the boat was, remembered Calamity wanted to marry me, "NO, I am not a monkey," I screamed into the Ether.

"YJ&%GJU"," suddenly freezing, must be a ghost here," the alien and stopped what he intended to do, obtain Lizzy's DNA to make a dozen hybrids to send back to Planet Earth so, Earth populated by his dozen handsome siblings, then no one would mind the aliens coming; coming for what? To conquer us and be kind, caring, benevolent rulers that never lied or played golf.

"&YJ*^%?" The handsome alien coming to terms a ghost was possessing him, and when he saw an ape in a bikini in his mind, ran screaming down miles of corridors, so upset was he, forgot the caddies so became exhausted, collapsing in a heap gasping for air, now useless as a boyfriend.

I came too, with no idea where or what I was supposed to do, until Calamity sent an S.O.S. to my mind. "Calamity I am coming," is not that you would say, or "I am on the loo sorry," "So what, I am fasting," "I am bathing the dog," replies to choose from?

"Lizzy, it is I, Henry, I have come to rescue you, my lifeboat is yonder," I said heroically, and Calamity flew into my arms as Lizzy ran to the lifeboat.

Later, "Lizzy, what about the others, I need to go save them?" I asked her to show a good side to me, caring, willing to self-sacrifice for others.

"What others?" She asked quite willing to let me die for others, but I was already dead, so turned to go and paused. Lizzy was right, what others, "Peter? Sorry no room in the lifeboat, all seats reserved for children.

"He pulled off my expensive false toenails, no one holds me by the toes."

"Steve?" He had already left with the alien Igor. And looked at Lizzy, 'I paid him back for pulling my hair, no one pulls my hair.'

"Fax," and saw the look in Lizzy's eyes, 'no one cheats on me.'

No one mentioned or remembered Oli and Jamie, they were extras and a ride in a spaceship was a bonus and need not save for a ticket on a 'Virgin' or 'Amazon' tourist spaceship. This was free, meals provided, women too in a LABORATORY, loo paper unfortunately was not as these aliens did not use toilets, waste was mental.

Now, Lizzy stood staring at the rows of buttons to press to launch the lifeboat. A meteor passed bumping the spaceship, so Lizzy, "Oh My God no," as she lurched forward with fingers sprayed open, and God replied, "Yes," as Lizzy's fingers hit and played 'chop sticks' on the rows of buttons.

I wondered if as she was about to join me in the After Life, then truly a romantic affair as I showed her red moons from the back of a winged horse, fed her heavenly pizza slices to a chorus of obo music, but all dreams vanished, spoofed just like that. Calamity read my mind, old jealousies surfaced, Calamity hit buttons.

There was a vibration, a motor coughed alive, "IJ&*&^GH," "Seat belts on," as the lifeboat glowed with fluorescent lights.

Then we were in space, alone until a cabinet opened and a drone appeared, "^*HUUY^?" "Drink service."

"Well Lizzy, just us again," I am meaning us two ignoring an ape.

She opened her mind to me, seeing me and did not smile. "What do you take me for, a bed jumper, tramp?"

"Ook," Calamity agreeing with her, "Ook," "tramp."

Lizzy mentally went wild, physically she tried to rip seats out of their lifeboat positions. "Mm," I thought, and should have remained silent but, "No, Fax was a past fling at the doorbell, I was the fling, but now you have a chance to see the real me."

She managed to rip the seats apart.

I drifted out into space, looking back seeing Calamity at a porthole making rude faces at me. Calamity the winner, "You monkey, me human," I thought back to her, and Lizzy had help taking her emotions out on the structures of the lifeboat that sped by.

At Planet Neptune I ventured to a porthole to peek in as all was silence.

Lizzy was sitting on a seat put back, she had been crying, there was no sign of Calamity. I was about to enter when, "Ok," "Monkey am I?" That ape bumped me away to the Ether.

"Ook," "ha, he," Calamity not crying but in a rabid chimpanzee mood.

Lizzy's clairvoyant mind awoke, "Henry, I am sorry," and went to the porthole and looked out, I waved back, she gave a little wave back then retreated, the face of a tormented bushbaby appeared, Calamity needed to accept I was not marrying her.

There was still a flame between Lizzy and me.

"And Cain killed his brother," so the first recorded murder, and Calamity knew if I was dead, then Lizzy could never have me, and so the apes love for me turned to sour cheese.

"Calamity stop," I asked of my friend, as Calamity tried to throttle me dead.

When that failed, she thought of knives and cleavers and used them, but they just tickled me.

The sun was hot so, she thought me there, but I thought myself away from her.

"Ook," "Where did he go?" Calamity asking herself.

"Lizzy, we must find a mate for Calamity to get peace," I told Lizzy back at the lifeboat, she agreed so I thought of Earth and the boat turned in the direction of home.

Then a giant spaceship passed us, the turbulence throwing Lizzy about, so she ended up with a mist atop of her, "Hello Henry," her exact words.

Chapter 12 Homeward

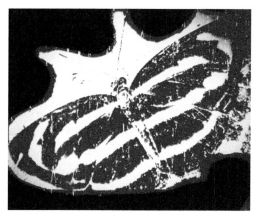

Figure 12 rare 1904 photo Borneo butterfly. Steven could not pin these creatures to a board as they were just that, creatures, but later ate his way through the Insect Kingdom.

A spaceship had a new crew, Captain Oli and his crew Jamie and Maria the Oliphant. It happened; thus, without drugged candles the humans became their normal dominant selves.

"I do not like being told what to do by anyone, especially little green men," Peter lounging on a swivel chair smoking home-made tobacco from strange plants found in the LABORATORY.

Peter picked up scalpels and threatened the attendants, "Take me to your leader," so took him to the Boss Alien woman. Peter was handsome and Boss Alien, fed up with looking at females, apart from the alien Mr. Handsome in 'Y' fronts, the only male alien seen.

"^HGG&&)," "I surrender, ravish me barbarian" and Peter threw her over a shoulder, she could floss his teeth later, and his boots needed polished, his hair gelled, the hairs sticking out of his nostrils trimmed, his fingernails emptied of boogiemen.

"I miss that idiot Steve, but never mind have this former alien Boss here to sweep up my ash.

"YUYHGF," the alien Boss, "This idiot has not learned to speak our alien difficult tongue, so does not know we are plotting our FREEDOM."

"Mm," this tobacco I can market on Earth and be mega rich," Peter seeing strange things and feeling he was getting smaller places.

"Ihkjkjhf7", "I could overpower this human twerp anytime, I just like the way he bosses me and his hair smells of honey, and", Peter walked into the control room, where an oliphant saw him, about turned, and gassed him, then trumpeted in his ears.

On the floor gassed aliens now dreaming of other worlds without Oliphant's.

"Hello whoever you are, I am Captain Oli, and this is my crew, Jamie," to Peter.

Peter looked at the oliphant and knew he needed a taxidermist to gain control of the ship. As if reading his mind, they say animals can, the Oliphant gassed Peter again.

"TYKUUBOUHOYGU," "Do not worry my love, I will take care of you," the Boss alien and summoned GIRLS to lead Peter to a lifeboat, as the Boss's quarters were behind that oliphant.

Any lifeboat, yes, so, Peter thrown aboard lifeboat number six, and crumpled under the life belt box, asleep, he had been gassed twice remember.

And Boss alien went to summon her girls and take back control of the ship, she did see Peter later with a chess set.

"Ha Ho ha, like to see them try," an oliphant mind reading Boss's mind as say elephants are telepathic, and in the miles of corridors, Maria, the oliphant marched with Jamie keeping order in the ranks. Behind them a handsome alien male in tight printed 'Y' fronts with pictures of kittens. In one hand a shovel and the other a big canvas black bag for oliphant accidents.

"H F B j& (88", "Wait till our alien revolution, then we change jobs," the alien only male abord ship so far.

An elephant trumpeted.

And on the moon two lovers had eaten all the bags of insects including the bags and were down to last insect.

"My love you can have the last," Steve lying, waiting to distract Igor and eat.

"&*(*&*^&," "Thank you, you have the last love," Igor waiting to eat it the minute Steve needed a pee, behind a hill made of moon cheese. Eating insects only and lacking other minerals produces L.S.D. effects, so the moon was cheese.

Unfortunately, Steve and Igor hated cheese, all types, blue, cheddar, Brie, Steve's socks, if it was cheese.

So down to the last insect.

"Look a spaceship," Steve seeing the ship approaching.

Igor ate the insect.

Steve looked back and was horrified to see nothing to eat. His tummy wobbled and he gassed.

"TUUT," "What a stink?" Igor complained and Steve mentally collapsed and went for her tummy, an easy thing to do as these green aliens never wore clothes.

"Ha he Ho," Igor giggled thinking Steve was playing games till he began to gnaw.

"THGGF?" "What are you doing idiot?" Igor.

"You ate the last insect, you lied, I want my insect," Steve and so WAR broke out on the moon over food resources.

For ammunition, handfuls of cheese to throw at each other.

There was the sound of the heavens coming apart, a tremendous roar, stars falling from the universe, planets colliding.

"We are about to die," Steve remembering all his bad deeds and could not remember a good thing he done and remembered,

"He loved Peter."

"!87Hyu6u?" Igor asking, "Are you gay or worse, a drag queen after my undies?" But Steve took her literally and could not find her undies as these aliens wore nothing.

So, Steve cheered remembering how he saved Peter in so many adventures.

"^*&^%%," "I must save my babies," Igor clutching her tummy and stopped speaking, why that was her spaceship, and it had stopped, and she was thinking of excuses to blame it all on Steve, "$%^," "his fault, he was so handsome".

A metallic stairwell descended from the hull of the ship; shadows followed by shadowy figures.

Were they aliens or humans?

"*UUJJN," "he forced me to go with him, thanks for rescuing me, he has a one-track mind, he just wants to eat insects and me, look at the teeth marks on my belly, I am pregnant, I have a hundred babies in my tummy," and that was a lot for, "*UUJJN".

Alien or human, those under the helmets needed to breath air so, kept them on.

Does that mean Steve and Igor were dead making cheese sandcastles?

Not all, we just forgot to mention they had helmets to, unless you were a ghost as you were already dead, but after eating all that cheese constipated, even emergency surgery to remove all that holiday rock, and because they were hallucination imagined all the flavors possible in that rock. They also needed tooth replacement trying to chew lumps of granite, pulled apart by skinless fingers, for the rocks were rough.

"I**&&HGGY," came from under one helmet.

"Steve pal," from under the other helmet.

"Master," Steve running to the space suit, "Sorry," Peter zooming away with a rocket backpack, for he believed he was holy, Jesus had told him to be friends with these aliens and take them back to Earth. Peter, we have seen been praying lots, "Jesus has commanded me to start a new religion for America," Peter seeing an end to the Mormon sect.

People did bow and grovel at his feet because he was a prophet of The Lord, if not the aliens did zap them.

Now Igor ran to Boss under the other helmet who held out a left hand to smooch, but where, every finger had a gem ring, the wrist gold bangles.

"$^^YYB&YG," meaning "now you have kissed my hand lick it cleans for I am the Primus of Intergalactic Love, and Peter my prophet." And mumblings came from Igor's tummy alerting The Boss someone was pregnant.

"THHJU&," otherwise, "the first children of the new super species."

And Steve ran past into the spaceship looking for a toilet as that cheese needed out, and was in luck, one of the first acts of friendship and Intergalactic |Love, was to build toilets and a plumbing system, waste tanks and a sewage plant staffed by I4ed waste disposal workers.

"Look Jamie, a hundred-dollar bill flushed down the loo," Oil blowing on the cash to dry it.

"Look Oli, a diamond ring," Jamie pulling off loo paper then flashing it on a finger, all found in smelly waste.

And an oliphant was happy too as it had unlimited mud baths in the sewage tank.

"And they can stay down there" I told Calamity as Lizzy floated by in flowing silks, now a High Priestess of the new religion and looked at Calamity for Lizzy carried a serrated knife that burglars use.

"Ook," Calamity not liking this religion.

"I need blood, the blood of a monkey to appease my wrath,"

Peter had spoken for Intergalactic Love earlier, and forgotten Calamity was an ape does not monkey.

Something not right here, Peter now a prophet of Love wanting rid of Calamity a nemesis?

"I like Solomon the Great will summon demons to build my temple in the Mohave Desert and need a ghost to go so he'll and fetch me Roger, a demon controller," oh yeh, something not right here, and had forgotten to mention the name of the ghost to go to hell but had narrowed his eyes and looked at my orb.

"HGGUYU&" The alien Boss, "if this what it takes to have harmony between the species."

I chocked and Calamity burst out in ape laughter, sounds like, "Okpoko, Ook, Ook, ha ho ha."

"Madam do you know who Roger is?" And was about to illuminate her but Peter rudely interrupted, "Lock them up and throw them to the wild beasts in the auditorium for my entertainment."

Auditorium, what wild beats? Then heard an oliphant trumpet so orbed away down miles of corridors to escape, rest and recreation exercises as calamity went to the hologram room and found sixteen chimps to feed her grapes, pick her fleas and plead marriage while she yawned uninterest.

"Lizzy, that idiot Peter is planning to bring Roger back to Earth with these aliens, and why are you waving that serrated dagger burglars use?" Behind her Fax lay stretch across a table, his chest exposed, snoring. "You are not, are you?"

Lizzy drew a red 'x' on his chest with lipstick, taking care to warm it with her hot breath and hotter lips.

"Mummy," I trembled in my orb, then decided right must come first over getting rid of the competition, 'Everything is fair in love and war.'

"Do not be daft Henry, I do not want fed to the wild beasts,

Steve is back you know?" Lizzy replied bending the serrated rubber knife.

"What about him?" I asked.

"Drugged, a woman must have ways to get her house keys back, her snips of hair, toenail cuttings and belly button fluff collection back, for no one cheats on Lizzy," and stuffed all these items down her elastics.

Then she put a hand into my orb and squeezed a cheek. "Huma ma pupa," I mumbled, I was worse than Steve fed a roach in honey sauce.

"Love me still, Henry," Lizzy asked.

"You bet," looking for the light switch and a laundry chute to slide Fax down.

"Then you must separate Roger from the Alien Boss and toss him out of this spaceship, time he visited Roger," here was the Lizzy of old that took care of badmen on a boat. Them or humanity was at stake. "I will handle Boss alien, I have a friend here," and I became manly suspicious, a female crew of three and one male in leopard 'Y' Fronts, and Fax asleep puckered his lips and smooched Lizzy's cheeks, which resulted in flushing Fax down the sideways elevator to deposit him anywhere but here, to the crew quarters, the Alien Boss fold down bed, the new sewage works, or out the exhaust as Jesus said, "What comes in goes out", so even this space ship wasted radioactive waste particles.

He did awake in soft beds with pink pillows, and curtains of male alien prints pulled closed, and when he walked away into the miles of corridors would notice his feet were nice and warm, and look down, and see he was in floozy red fluffy slippers so would scream.

The first scream of the revolution to rid the spaceship of Roger and Boss alien.

*

Now Fax always believed in himself, why he kicked off the floozy pink slippers and headed to the control room to take over this ship, he was of New York's Finest, the bravest of them all, and when he passed Boss Alien room was amazed to see a fold down camp bed, and instead of a mattress little stone, human toenail clippings, dried sea urchins, biting red ants, still alive.

"This yours," amazing this alien could speak human all this tongue, and held up his police bronze badge, bigger than his comrades as was at the bottom of a cornflake box.

"That your bed?" Fax spell bound a woman was tougher than him or mentally instable, then she began to oscillate between no anatomy and human female shape, she needed clothes, but that was the idea to captivate this weak minded human to be her warrior against Peter.

Afterwards he could regulate to look after that oliphant, and then she asked herself, "Why do we need an oliphant?"

Then she showed Fax with a click of a finger a double sized bed with all the trimmings, even a wall television showing the American Presidential Election to put Fax into a brilliant mood. She was wrong, it brought out the beast in Fax and forgetting his Lizzy threw the Alien Boss onto that bed and jumped in, lucky for her she shifted as he landed, sprung up to hit the ceiling, then back on the bed and sprung off again onto a human bear skin rug, where Fax moaned and groaned.

"Let doctor Alien Boss mend your broken bones," and with a mental thought, dimmed the lights and put on soothing bagpipe music as she had watched the New York police Pipe Band.

Fax tried to cover his ears but found an alien tongue deep inside licking out ear wax, and it was so ticklish Fax forgot Lizzy completely, the sour cream.

*

"I summon you Chief Roger," Peter over his microphone, so all heard it aboard ship, for Peter was modern people, so dispensed with queasy boards and tarot carrots, he was Peter the Great, all he had to do was use this microphone and Roger miles below did hear and come.

But what Peter did not understand about the Ether was its dimensions existed next to each other.

Roger was next to him, and Peter never saw him, just blamed passing Oli and Jamie talking the Oliphant for a walk for the sudden bad essences.

"Hello Peter, my boy," Roger whispered into Peter's right ear, so Peter jumped out of his skin. Now Peter could see Roger and what the Outer darkness had done to his good looks, rotted them, and he stunk of cheap meths as alcoholics crammed Roger's new home and were generous so shared with Roger.

 Peter handed Roger a mirror, there was a high pitch scream as Roger recognized himself as evil, "The King of Rottenness," and he was proud and now be invited to European royal weddings.

AND THE SPACESHIP entered Earth's unseen electric ionosphere that fizzled with electromagnetic power, home of WHITE NOISE and proven by Tulsa, free electricity, but electrified all living things on that ship.

Peter showed his X-ray innards to Roger who was amazed Peter had an extra kidney, which made him think of circus wonders, "Where is my beloved Steve?"

Yes, where was Steve, ah, here he was, summoned by an inner call, on his way to Roger and Master Peter, pushing a pram full of a hundred baby Steve's, behind followed Igor pushing another pram full of warm bottles of milk and clean diapers.

Behind them Oli pushing another pram slowly filling with soiled diapers. Behind Oil came an Oliphant guarding her two human friends.

Behind her came Jamie pushing another pram filling with oliphant banana fuel

Until electrified, then an oliphant went berserk for it loved Jamie and Oli.

"That was great Alien Boss" Fax now out of his electrified mood, thinking it was his new girlfriend that put him in paradise; fat chance Fax, just wet a couple fingers and stick them in a wall socket.

"What is that STINK," the Alien Boss pushing Fax out into the miles of corridors in the double bed as was a wheelie bed, could slap shut too, and capable of speeds of a hundred miles per hour as had a little fusion motor, Fax beware.

And the three other alien girl crew gathered about Boss Alien giggling mentally to each other for Fax was naked, only a lily flower covering his bum as he lay on his stomach, yes on his stomach as this is not a porno story.

And Alien Boss using mental remote control had the bed follow her and her armed crew.

Armed with serrated burglar daggers Lizzy had given them, oh dear, from Lizzy?

And looking for Lizzy an alien male squeezed into an American flag print tight 'Y' Front. Lizzy had hypnotized him so he worshipped her, she was unlike alien girls, she had thingmabobs that male aliens dreamed off, but since girls' rule, would stay dreams.

"I must throw Peter off this ship as if Lizzy hates you, so do I," and that explains why he had it in for Peter.

Which means me, Henry and Calamity were safe.

*

"Have I done the right thing; oh, Jesus help me do what is right?" Peter not happy Roger calling himself 'KING.' He wanted to be king, he needed help to send Roger back to the Outer Darkness. He heard angelic harp music, an alien angel had read his thoughts, she needed an invitation, the question was, had Peter invited her?

"Nope," for Roger believed he was greater than Light, not his fault, just down in the lower energy levels of heaven, all that meth drinking and listening to drunks boast they could knock Mohammed Ali out blindfolded, win the American Presidential Election sober, douse with a twig and find Texan oil, have melissa Trump leave Donald for a Cuban fling, yes, Roger believed his own boast, "I am Zeus", so wanted to get back to Earth, possess the likes of Steve and have him become the King of Samoa, and rule people, and from Samoa America by infiltrating Fox News.

Yes, Roger had become a megalomanic, a cheap meths addict, which was lethal since he was in hell.

"Peter never mentions Jesus when I am here do you understand," and Roger demonstrated his power by breathing upon Peter, now overcome and dizzy with meth fumes fell backwards onto the ship controls.

Every knob, and there was two hundred Peter managed to hold and move, the steering wheel he spun, the foot pedals he used, and pressed the "DO NOT PRESS2 red button as was in alien pobblebonks.

Lo, the ship landed with an electric hum on the manicured lawn of the White House as a garden party was in full swing.

I am telling you the truth, and why this story was amongst the UFO files below that building for years, till the public had access to UFO and conspiracy files there.

"What the blazes?" The President at the time.

"Shot it down," the Secretary of Defense at the time.

"They might have COVID, burn the lot," The Health Secretary at the time.

"Is that an alien hulk squeezed into zebra 'Y' Front? The president's wife asked ogling.

Just how did the only male alien aboard ship manage to be the first one out, it happened thus, no idea as was not there.

Just that Steve opened the control ,room door just as the ship went hair wry, throwing him and his hundred baby stevens on Peter who went berserk when he awoke, fleeing the room, seeking a life boat shouting, "Jesus, I prayed to you and you answer me thus," blaming the Lord when should be giving thanks, as was away from that foul beathed spirit, Roger, whose attitude changed seeing all these baby Steve's.

"Oh," he crooned as Steven was his favorite adopted son, "To blazes with Peter," Roger added for effect.

"Hello Peter, it was Lizzy, join us?" Lizzy outside the control room holding a burning sage stick, a rosary, and bottle of Blessed Holy Water 1660 vintage.

Peter stopped, he was looking at Fax rolling along on a bed, pushed free by alien girls.

Peter, Lizzy, and company watched Fax go, into the control room. Fax looked so happy sleeping well, no one had it in them to waken him, but Roger did.

"I am one of New York's Finest," and Fax stuck his bronze badge the Buddhist Dai Lama had blessed as Fax had been his security officer.

And The Monkey King appeared in Roger's orb and kicked Roger to an approaching angel, yes, the female variety that fouls you thinking you are in heaven while she is bundling you to HELL.

And she kicked Roger's orb back and the Monkey King being a monkey kicked Roger AWAY, just as Oli and J\amie appeared, and an Oliphant and Roger got stuck somewhere.

What a trumpet that oliphant blared as now gas was building up places where Roger was.

"I repent," Roger screamed seeing bananas coming his way in

a green cloud.

"Ook," The Monkey King jumping about wanting peanuts excited by Roger's discomfort.

"Did I hear righty?" The female angel craning to hear Roger's confession.

"Ook," Calamity seeing The Monkey King and fell in love again.

"Ook," The Monkey King seeing Calamity and about to what, who knows, he was The Monkey King, pure mischief and at the same time, he had a bright soul.

That is when Boss Alien squeezed past the oliphant and reached the controls.

"Please remove the Oliphant as it is sitting on the starter button and the gear stick is stuck places," she pleaded all the wind of war blown out of her by an Oliphant.

And her three-girl crew backed away fearing they did have to spit and polish the controls the oliphant sat upon, as Oli and Jamie no longer worked for them, but freelanced.

And Lizzy vanished, "Where did she go?" I asked alarmed, what hidden horrors did this ship hold, sixteen-legged pink octopus, land sharks running about on ten legs, racoons seeking rubbish, so forgetting I was just a FLING, was alarmed for Lizzy, those racoons had bad breath eating trash.

"Jackie Chan, you have my address, and remember I like four cheese pizzas, strawberry perfumes, strawberries too, turquoise necklaces and a gold address neck clip for the cat, see you at mine, bye," and fueled the male alien in to tight 'Y' Fronts that now threatened to burst with a slobbering smooch.

Then kicked him out a convenient EXIT green fire door.

"GJJUYTY", him outsides seeing hundreds of men in black surrounding The President, AND IN English, that he had forgotten he could speak, "Do not shoot, take me to your leader, I am called Jackie Chan by that terrific woman back there the red head with green eyes and breathing moving chest that makes men her captives," and yes, all that in, "GJJUYTY".

"BANG," it was, the oliphant gassing and out came Roger at a million miles an hour, right past Peter, and the last seen heading towards the jungles of the Congo, an angel hot on his orb trail, as angels never give up. This was corrupted by the Royal Mounted Police of Canada to, "We always catch our man", which is sexist as evil rotten ladies exist scheming to have men one after another if they gave presents.

Does this sound like my Lizzy, 'C888' yes, but the difference is, these women voted for the opposite party you voted for, so were truly past the sell by date?

Now Peter seeing an open window skedaddled down a drainpipe on the ship's hull, and slipped on sea gull droppings, oh dear the ship's hull was a thousand feet high and so wide, faded in the distance, ,but as Peter fell, "Jesus I am sorry, save me now," and the rotten soul was caught by three alien girls escaping from cleaning duties, and together ran into nearby rose bushes and much screaming was heard as roses have thorns, and the alien girls do not need clothes, and Peters clothes were soon ripped from him, again.

Then a bed thrown out with a human man waving a light, "It is a hairy Yeti, in pink slippers, it has a laser pointed at us, shot to kill boys and girls," the leader of The Men in Black and opened fire.

You see, the human search lights were bouncing off fax's police shield, producing beams of light that "I am blinded, the F****** alien blinded me, shot to kill boy and girls", again the leader of the men in black.

"I am out of here," Fax and with rapid foot movements had his bed in wheels moving, and downhill would you believe so was in downtown city traffic in no time, with an army of Men in Black shooting running after him, as none thought Fax could out pace them.

They were wrong, Jesus prayed to so much, he let Fax's bed roll in front of the Bronx over night bus and he was away at sixty miles per hour.

"Weeeee," the idiot allowing the Jetstream to part the gel in his hair.

To rustle his hairy chest, to bring essences and then pongs of America to his nostrils, and fizzy drink cans thrown at him from the cars up front.

"F7777777", gay and pinged lit weeds at him that singed Fax's curly chest he used a curler on.

"The bum is getting away, where are the cars, whose got the car keys?" The Men in Black leaderless as their leader was back up the hill assuring the president the alien on the levitating bed would be dissected.

"Judas, they are tiny," The President seeing one hundred babies run out of the ship onto his manicure front lawn he used for putting golf, and they were half alien, so ripped clumps of Earth up and threw it at the humans giggling, then cleared off onto the bushes.

Tell you, these bushes better be large, and yes cousins of Oli and Jamie's cut them, explains why bushes looked like strange Aztec deities?

And just when The Men in Black were reloading an oliphant charged out amongst them, scattering them, bulldozing the cars, stopping to eat the fruit in the fruit punches, then Jamie and Oil jumped off and filled up takeaway box with food, as those aliens ate with their minds. Thinking up hot dogs for these two cleaners out of thin air.

"We need SWAT here, get them, I want that elephant stuffed on my desk by the morning", Mr. President but the oliphant was too quick, and as an oliphant never forgets, was making for the zoo in New York.

"We are here for the ride and have nowhere else to go as unwanted immigrants," Oli explains and Jamie nods agreement eating an extra hot tortilla he took from the garden party. "Gasp, water," we leave Jamie pleading, "Silly, if we stop, we will be caught" Oli, so off they went a jolly threesome.

"Stay and come we us back home," the Boss Alien ogling Lizzy and suddenly I Henry, realized why it was an all-girl crew.

"Lizzy, I love you," I gasped and showed myself to the Boss Alien as an angry demented ghost.

"Got you," an angel from no where and dragged me away.

"Sorry, I must go, I love men to much," Lizzy and smooched the Boss to keep things on a friendship level. Then she daintily skipped hopped and somersaulted out a closed window so, was easy prey for Steve to pick her up, gloatingly chuckling into a spare McClaren expensive silver pram and was away before Igor, said, "How can you desert me after I ruined my figure giving you a hundred children?"

"|That is why I am off, you keep them," and Steve ran down the gang plank.

"Caught one, Judas they are ugly," a Man in Black looking at Steve with a dozen carbines stuck up his nose.

"Take him to Area 51, they will know what to do with IT," The Chief Man in Black and Steve was put into Helicopter Air Force Three, the personnel machine of the president's wife, for her to go shopping and buy a thousand p[airs of purple shoes, to visit her tennis coach, a gamer she loathed, and to personally teach chosen Men in Black how to fly on autopilot.

"Are you real?" The President's wife asked Steve poking his grotesque stomach from which a roach ran up from the helicopter floor.

"Mm," a carpet cleaner to boot, very handy, I shall call you "Calamity," the wife of The President peeking under Steve's elastic, well rumors had it they were huge, was she in luck, was she about to recruit a private teacher on U.F.O.'s.

The helicopter door opened, and a body thrown out.

Never mind, Steven would not go to Area 51 for dissection, instead he fell into a vacant cage in the New York Zoo, 'YETI', written badly on a sign above.

Now, aboard ship Igor took over control at a hundred miles up, she cried so much promising HELL as hell has no fury as a woman scorned.

"Will go back and find this rotter Steve, that Oliphant made a lot of banana mess about ship, and no one messes with one of my girls and gets away with it," Alien Boss with a steel glint in her eyes.

*

Scratch further down Jackie Chan," Lizzy telling her new butler what to do, and he was happy, he had FREEDOM, a day off a week to visit China Town where he was making a film, soon to be released as the 'Karate Alien from Out There,' this coming Halloween.

Yes, Lizzy was happy, presents were piling up at her door, and suitor calling cards a mountain off on the other side under the mailbox.

She thought of old times, of Roger, how a handsome man could allow badness to change himself into an ugly troll. Lizzy wondered what presents he was nice he might have brought her. News columns on how talented she was, that would certainly get him in her house, but how far?

Where was he now, did that Angel Marshall catch up with him, he was last seen heading for the Congo, where he did feel at home, crocodiles, oliphants, apes, monkeys, snakes, war, and cheap hotels with no running water to remind him of the jungles of Borneo, home, or was The Netherlands his home, who knows, who really cares, not Lizzy and remembered:

Peter, another handsome man, yes, Lizzy liked handsome men and saddened Peter was a rotter, then cheered, she was up to the challenge of saving him, anything once, you never lived until you tried.

She remembered the dare to swim to Cuba and followed by the press and sharks and was suddenly famous overnight as the nude FREEDOM swimmer. A girl to become a top New York vet had to use her assets and Lizzy did.

She remembered the oliphant, that same beast in love with Jamie and Oli, had swallowed a chili peanut some kid had tossed it, and went berserk, and it was Lizzy in a bikini top and standard green jungle uniform shorts that, atop a taxi put sixteen tranquilizers into the oliphants bum, then leapt from a yellow cab roof onto the head of the oliphant.

"Dreamies," Lizzy shaking a bag of humbugs and steered the oliphant back to the zoo. The next day she was on the cover of 'Times,' 'Vogue' 'Private Eye' 'Playboy' and the gifts moored and parked at aerodromes or car show rooms.

She remembered me, and with sadness her heart broke, it had been more than a fling, it was true love, and 'Bo Ho', Lizzy cried remembering gossip that that 'bl****angel' had taken me to HELL, and not Roger in the Congo learning the skills of a Vet detective so he could masquerade as a physical.

"Ook," and Calamity appeared and 'Bo Ho,' joined Lizzy for the monkey missed me, she had no one to throw rotten figs at, and from Spirit Calamity produced a solid 'quizzer board.' "Ook," "Henry here."

So, Lizzy cheered and put an empty beer bottle on the board instead of a glass. She was mourning for her memories, a good reason to drink oneself to emergency.

Calamity narrowed eyes and "I want a drink too."

"Oh, Calamity go buy your own," Lizzy replied, and the ape went bananas.

Peace descends as Calamity with a box of famous American beer beside her started the game.

Lizzy with a steak over an eye joined in asking for me.

"Come get your monkey back Henry," she told the board.

It was only a loud long alcoholic burp that saved Lizzy as by the time finished, Calamity was gasping for air and forgotten the primate insult.

From the Ether I saw the empty beer bottle and moved it spelling HENRY is here "Ook."

Seeing the Angel Marshall approaching panic gripped me, I had to get away, The Ether had made a mistake, I belonged topside, not down here with addicts showing me their massive collet ions of porno, paracetamols, and stuffed olives.

"I never make a mistake," the Angel Marshall flapping her wings nearing, but I was out, inside that empty beer bottle.

And the Ether groaned, a mistake had been made, another Henry Adamson had been murdered in Sandakan, Iowa, 1905.

"I never made a mistake," The Angel Marshall retreating to The Hall of Records, and sure enough, I belonged to level three, with the billions of other souls, that same level of light energy Saint Paul visited and spoke to angels, like her.

Now the angel sat on a log and rested a chin on a palm, with knees up in deep contemplation over her mistake.

She had missed Roger.

To go back empty handed was an admission of failure.

 She did have to go on a quest in the physical to catch Roger.

She hated the physical, it was full of educated persons crammed into toilets at garden parties sniffing cocaine.

She hated the physical as supermarkets reduced food that in a few hours did be unsafe to eat, and in those few hours it took you to get home, then empty the cat litter, stuff plastic money into the electric meter, then get around to eating that food, you got a new bill from emergency for food poisoning the whole family, ten kids, both sets of grandparents but no husband, he was living with a floozy down town who worked nights to keep him happy playing expensive console games.

Yes, the Angel Marshall hated Earth and was in deep s*** for screwing up, they did pluck her feathers one by one, and it did take two years to complete the baldness, and all did repent, and she did return to her job a better angel.

An angel wanting Revenge.

"I am in here Lizzy," me speaking to Lizzy and before Lizzy could rejoice and hug and kiss the bottle an ape grabbed it and went out the open window and drifted up another sixteen flights on the steel fire escape ladder to the roof.

Behind her sprinting up was Lizzy, all that heavy drinking having no effect on her health as she was a WONDER WOMAN who exercised daily. Two hundred press ups and a hundred-yard sprint round the apartment building, then a jog up sixteen flights of stairs to her level, and each bullet hole she saw, was reminded of Steve, not me.

Anyway, on the roof thousands of disturbed pigeons roosting in huts took alarm over Calamity and flew up pumping phosphate upon her orb, so it grew heavy and smelly for calamity, so she dropped the beer bottle, and it broke, and I knew FREEDOM.

"Henry, I love you," Lizzy at last on the roof.

And then out of the shadows Peter appeared with Steve at his side, "Oh how cute," Peter said aiming a handgun at Lizzy as Steve playing with rope to bind Lizzy up got near her, yes, near her but no nearer.

Beer bottles dropped smash with nasty serrated edges the maker of burglar serrated knives could copy and make a 'BOWIE 'of a serrated burglar knife and be famous as did appear on the MOST WANTED list.

So, Steve whose feet had flattened and splayed only wore the top of shoes, not the soles for comfort, and "eek"," oh" "Christ""" phone 111"" master I am dying" that sort of rubbish.

Peter mesmerized by Steve's dance, Steve collided with him and took them both over the top of the building, thirty-two levels up.

Lizzy ran to look; all she saw was darkness and car lights below and the faint sounds of arguments of pedestrians.

No spat, yes, two splats but more like thuds as landed in a passing rubbish lorry on the way to landfill.

"Better make sure they do not come back Calamity, figs in it for you," I said, and Calamity vanished.

"Nice move Henry," Lizzy sweeping the beer bottle remains off the top of the roof. She kept seeping, she was nervous, the cat meowed in the pile of dust, the rat it was after squeaked there, a pet escaped baby cobra hissed there, a Dominoes Mushroom pizza still hot in a box Lizzy took after flicking the bay cobra on the nose to be silent.

"Pizza Henry, Lizzy drooling, "Oh forgot," and swept the dust over the roof.

Dominoes Mushroom always put Lizzy into a romantic mood.

I ate mine in the Ether, oysters instead of mushrooms.

I gazed into her eyes, she gazed into my orb.

With a fling, Lizzy sent the empty pizza box somewhere, knocking out thousands of pigeons that fell thirty-two levels to the pedestrians below.

Curses floated up about pigeon pooh and allergic to feathers, but do not worry, the birds were extras hired for a barrow of grain swept up off the silo floor when emptied to make Corn Flakes.

They were happy birds as flew away to gorge themselves on

the rest of that grain, poohing as they flew for |The Creator Spirit made them that way, FREEDOM of diapers and too tight underwear.

Yes, God is wise and Majestic.

"Henry, kiss me," Lizzy, thinking of what presents a ghost could give her.

Here ENDS the tale of a GHOST ROMANCE, a COMEDY MELEE.

Figure 13 Green crested lizard, Borneo, old Henry Adamson drawing, 1903.

ACKNOWLEDGEMENT

I acknowledge the words that tumble into my right temple and come out the right prose.

GHOST COMEDIES

"What, no you misunderstand, I am Peter," but he could call himself 'Handsome Prince Charming,' they still would rob, beat, steal his clothes, especially the stilettos and leave him in his lingerie's, as night workers were hygienic and did not wear another's unmentionables. And Steve went off behind the bushes with these two-night workers and the question is? Did Steve have rabies from a monkey eaten by a leopard and did he offer a packet of crispy chili roasted crickets to these girls, and another question, what explosive reply did these girls give him, our 'Igor' of the story?

Ghost Wife, A Comedy Of Errors

Oh, Morag dear, you died so do what ghosts do, Rest In Peace.
"not on your Nelly, I am very much alive, and stop ogling the medium Con, dear." Lots of madcap ridiculous fun. Information on the After Life, pity our world leaders would not stop and listen, might be no more wars.
Is comic mayhem, fanciful rubbish to tickle. The ghosts here will not haunt but make you laugh, so do not worry about holding bibles, these ghosts are clowns.

Ghost Romance

orangutan in tow. So, load up on bananas and figs as the ape eats non-stop.
"Ook," is her only word spoken.

Do not worry about the extras feeding the crocodiles, they come under a dime a dozen and are not in any union, and better, made of indigestible rubber.

Not to worry animal lovers, a vet is on standby by for the sweet crocodiles, sea water variety so bigger, nastier, fierce and wanting you as food.

This book speaks heaps for food out there, a mixture of local, Indian, Chinese, Portuguese, Dutch, British, you name it, it found a way onto the menu.

Come eat more than a banana and drink condensed tea milk to sweeten you up.

BOOKS BY THIS AUTHOR

Eagor The Monster

Non illustrated version.
84488 words 248 pages
A giant book of giggles.
The humorous tale of an ugly monster who
Is a cheat on his many girlfriends.
But he is so ugly?
He works for himself although signed up
to do jobs for the HOOD cousins.
Discount salespersons who will sell you what you
do not need, like granny who hunts were-wolfs
from her zoomed up mobile home.
A were-wolf girl with a pretty ankle who yes, is
 one of the ugly monsters' girls.
Come laugh meeting Eagor's other friends,
Such as Badbladder who dresses as Bunnykins,
In his effort to marry Princess Lana.
And the monster treats his friends bad, as
 gets Badbladder to do his job of pulling
twenty carts full of holidaying villagers on
The Blackhood express.
Giggle laugh snort meeting Eagor's enemies, Bear a chili
Addicted bear, Morag a frizzled-out witch, Wee Mary her apprentice
And a Glasgow hard case who knows how to deal with Eagor,
"Will you marry me monster," as Wee Mary is desperate.
Just a funny silly tale to brighten your day.

The Man

79586 words 419 pages Science Fiction Adventure War Horror Mammoth read.

illustrated.

Are we predestined, reborn?

Early Christian dogma had reincarnation as a core belief.

Until The Empress Theodora, A.D. 561 banned such an idea?

She wanted worshipped, decaled divine and a bust next to Julius and prayed to.

Oh well, tar la, LA, such is life, those above make the rules.

So, The Man is reborn again to pass or fail his lessons, depending on if he shows mercy or not?

Met his loves, Nesta whom he left on the spiritual plane.

Meet his friends, Tintagel the Clone who authored this book.

Meet The master Priest, a vampire firmly making this book a horror novel.

Meet aliens galore and realise we are not alone.

See the colours of space and wonder at the music of the stars.

Look and listen in The Man.-

Ants 169: non illustrated

Is ANTS (ILLUSTRATIONS without pictures. Intended for

Mungo, Books One And Two

97334 words 450 pages Science Fiction Adventure

A mammoth adventure for Mungo, the boy raised by lions on New Uranus, humanoid, all creatures here are about humanoid thanks to genetic engineering.

Of his first love, Sasha, daughter of Red Hide, King of Lions, to his war with Carman, Queen of Lizard Folk.

These lizard folk like humans at a barbecue, as the burgers, steaks, and sausages.

No wonder Mungo wars against them.

And no one wins in a war as a human star ship arrives and enslaves the lot.

Advanced humans see other humans as undesirables.

Run through the red grass, climb giant rhododendron flowers, smell the clean air of the mountains, and only found here with Mungo the lion rider.

Mungo, Book One.

50632 words, 201 pages.

Mungo travels his world to the floating city of Huverra.

Meet his friends and enemies.

Meet more mazarrats as they provide a parallel story.

Mazarrats a cross between a mongoose and a baboon is said.

Not true, they are cute singers looking for a home.

Mazarrats, you want to take home with you.

They run a story themselves between the lines.

Discover the technological wonders these lizard folks have.

Ants 169, Non Illustrated

ANTS 169 non illustrated Science Fiction Adventure Horror 82652 words 169 illustrations. 262 pages

(Illustrations being reduced to fit Kindle, under review)

Cross species genetic engineering.

The unseen power of Spirit.

Mammoth adventure with Luke of The Ants, a rival to Tarzan, whereas Tarzan was brought up on ape milk, Luke is raised on Black Ant milk.

Luke dances to the unseen spiritual power of the universe for strength. When he shows compassion, mercy he glows, otherwise he walks in revenge, darkness.

Sound familiar.

Amazing strength and he battles Insect Nobles for the dominant species on Planet World.

Humanoid Insects from chromosome splicing.

Human genes into insects to make them taller, handsome, attractive but cruel masters of Planet World.

A good hero needs a side kick, Luke has Utna, a giant Black Ant he rides, saves shoe leather. Come ride a giant ant with Luke. Let the breeze refresh you.

Look at the crimson moons, fill with him 'spring fever' and you are too.

Planet World, Ant Rider Book One, Illustrated.

Planet World, Ant Rider Book One, Illustrated.
Science Fiction Horror Adventure
Is Book One of Ants 169, 47619 words, 219 pages.
Ants 169 is so large needed halved.
Book One has Luke finding out his aims and becomes a hero by fighting for human rights.
Full, of adventure, example, Luke ends up a galley rower and saves the ship from pirates.
And like a dog, Utna pines for Luke wondering seashores seeking Luke, his friend, and like a dog, loves his master.
This book is about love, the power of it, it sings across space as Light. Be lit then.

Phoenix, Ant Rider Book Two, Illustrated.

Phoenix, Ant Rider Book Two, Illustrated.
Science Fiction Adventure Horror
Cross species genetic engineering.
Is concluding part of Ants 169
48439, 187 pages.
Luke concludes his epic struggle against the humanoid Insect Nobles, become this way by gene mixing.
The Insect Queen, Nina and he race to the star ship Phoenix, a human ship that crashed on Planet World in the Time of Myths. What secrets does it hold?

Is the Insect God Enil a human? One way to find out, come join Luke and be his friend.

Ants 169, Illustrated

ANTS 169 ILLUSTRATIONS SCIENCE FICTION HORROR
genetic engineering and gene splicing.
A spiritual side is we like the hero Luke, can obtain SPRING FEVER and do much with it.
82652 words 169 illustrations. 262 pages
(Illustrations being reduced to fit Kindle, under review)

Mammoth adventure with Luke of The Ants, a rival to Tarzan, whereas Tarzan was brought up on ape milk, Luke is raised on Black Ant milk.
Luke dances to the unseen spiritual power of the universe for strength. When he shows compassion, mercy he glows, otherwise he walks in revenge, darkness.
Sound familiar.
Amazing strength and he battles Insect Nobles for the dominant species on Planet World.
Humanoid Insects from chromosome splicing.
Human genes into insects to make them taller, handsome, attractive but cruel masters of Planet World.
A good hero needs a side kick, Luke has Utna, a giant Black Ant he rides, saves shoe leather. Come ride a giant ant with Luke. Let the breeze refresh you.
Look at the crimson moons, fill with him 'spring fever' and you are too.

Printed in Great Britain
by Amazon